Woodworking

with kids

ST·REMY MEDIA

St. Remy Media Inc.

President: Pierre Léveillé
Vice President, Finance and Operations:
    Natalie Watanabe
Managing Editor: Carolyn Jackson
Managing Art Director: Diane Denoncourt
Systems Director: Edward Renaud
Director, Business Development: Christopher Jackson
Marketing Coordinator: Monique Riedel

Woodworking with Kids

Senior Editors: Marc Cassini, Pierre Home-Douglas
Senior Editor, Production: Brian Parsons
Art Directors: Michel Giguère, Solange Laberge,
    Francine Lemieux, Robert Paquet, Odette Sévigny
Editor: Jim Hynes
Writers: Rob Labelle, Rob Lutes
Illustrators: Michel Giguère, Patrick Jougla,
    Robert Paquet
Photographer: Robert Chartier
Photo Research: Linda Bryant
Editorial Assistant: Aldo Parisi
Senior Research Editor: Heather Mills
Indexer: Linda Cardella Cournoyer
Production Coordinator: Dominique Gagné
Prepress Technician: Jean Angrignon Sirois
Scanner Operator: Martin Francoeur

*The following persons also assisted in the
preparation of this book:*
Kathryn Cole, Lorraine Doré, Joey Fraser,
Pascale Hueber

Consultants
Jon Arno, Stewart McLaughlin, Alan Ostroff,
Michael Saunders

ISBN 1-894827-26-0
COPYRIGHT © 2002, St. Remy Media Inc.

Printed in Canada

www.stremy.com

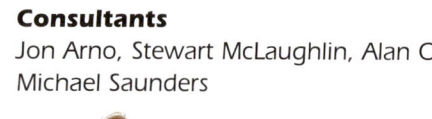

Woodworking

with kids

Table of

Contents

How to Use This Book

We went the whole nine yards to make sure you and your family have everything you need to build the woodworking projects in this book. Take a minute or two to read about the many features and tips we've provided to make your woodworking experience a safe and enjoyable one. The best tip we can offer is simple: Use your best judgment. No one knows a child better than the adults closest to him or her, so take some time to consider your young apprentice's age and skill level before starting a project. If you have any doubt about your child's ability to do one of the steps, err on the side of caution and do it yourself. Your assistant can learn a lot by watching you work.

Under the project title, a brief **introduction** outlines the project and helps you decide if it's right for you.

A brief description of how each project is assembled, complete with a detailed exploded-view **diagram** of pieces and measurements.

An estimate of the **time** required to build each project. The time will vary with the age and skill level of the builder.

134 | Building a Picture Frame | 135

No picture is quite complete without a frame. And this traditional wooden frame, with two kinds of decorative molding, is the perfect companion for your favorite photo or work of art. It also makes a great, creative gift.

The 1x3 pine used in this project is a good size for framing an 8x10 picture. The cove molding on the inside edges helps hold the picture in place and gives the frame a more decorative look. Corner molding on the outside finishes the edges, hides the fasteners, and adds a nice finishing touch.

Materials you'll need

Wood	5 feet 1x3 pine
	5 feet 1x1 molding
	4 feet ½-inch cove molding
Hardware	Small screw eyes and picture wire
	Picture pivots
Fasteners	#6 1½-inch screws
	¾-inch finishing nails
	1-inch finishing nails
Miscellaneous	Wood glue
	8x10 cardboard backing
	8x10 picture-frame glass

The time it takes

3 hours to build
1 hour to paint

How the pieces fit together...

• The 1x3 framing is held together by screws driven through the corners.

• Cove molding cut to fit the inside of the framing is glued and nailed in place.

• Corner molding is cut to fit around the framing and attached with nails.

• Pivots hold the picture, cardboard, and glass in place.

• The frame is hung with small screw eyes and picture wire.

Corner molding: top and bottom (2) 15½" x 1" x 1"

Corner molding: sides (2) 13⅝" x 1" x 1"

Cardboard 10" x 8"

Pivots (4)

Glass 10" x 8"

Framing: sides (2) 13" x 2½" x ¾"

Cove molding: sides (2) 8⅛" x ½" x ½"

Cove molding: top and bottom (2) 10" x ½" x ½"

Framing: top and bottom (2) 15" x 2½" x ¾"

Did You Know... **How to Choose Picture-Frame Glass and Mats**

If you'll be framing a watercolor painting or a photograph, protect and enhance it with a covering of glass. Nonglare glass is great for bright rooms, where sunlight can cause reflections. But for pictures that have a lot of detail, standard clear glass is the better choice.

If the picture you want to frame is a little too small, the space between it and the frame can be filled with a mat. Mats are made from a thick colored card that fits like a window around the picture. You'll find there's a wide variety of mat colors available. Choose one that doesn't draw too much attention away from the picture and fits well with the color of your frame and the painting or photograph it surrounds.

The tools you'll need...

Tape measure
Screwdrivers
Utility knife
Clamps
Putty knife
Awl
Hammer
Backsaw
Straightedge
Wire cutters
Miter box
Nail set
Electric drill with #6 combination bit

An easy-to-use list of all the **tools** used to build each woodworking project, complete with photos.

A list of all the **wood** and other **materials** you'll need for each project, right down to the length of boards and the size of fasteners and hardware.

Fun facts related to the project, from instructions on how to use it to recipes and interesting historical tidbits.

Adult's Corner...

Installing the bottom panel

12

Drilling pilot holes for the screws that secure the bottom panel can be tricky, especially for young woodworkers. The cleats on the side panels are narrow, so you'll have to hold the drill up close to the sides while you work. This can be a little awkward, so drill the holes yourself, holding the drill as straight as possible. Make sure to point out the importance of a steady hand and good positioning to your young apprentice. He or she can drive the screws in by hand once the pilot holes are made.

◆ Position the bottom panel on its cleats, then mark four evenly spaced points along each edge and three along each end. Offset the points by 3/8 inch from the side and end panels. Also offset them from the screws holding the bottom cleats in place.

◆ Drill a pilot hole into the bottom panel at each mark *(right)*. Then, drive 1-inch round-head screws into the holes to secure the bottom.

Adult's Corner tells you that a grown-up needs to perform the task in that step. Sometimes the skill or strength required makes a job too difficult for the young woodworker. If you have any doubt about the difficulty of *any* step, make it an Adult's Corner, too, and do it yourself!

Up Close...

Cutting the beanbag holes

◆ Clamp the front panel to the table with two of the holes overhanging the edge of the table. Fit the blade of a saber saw into an access hole and cut toward the marked line *(right)*.

◆ Cut halfway around the circle, guiding the saw slowly and carefully to keep the blade on line. Stop the saw, then reposition yourself to make it more comfortable to finish making the cut. Or, you can cut halfway around the circle then complete the cut by sawing in the opposite direction from the access hole.

◆ Cut the second hole, then shift and reclamp the board to cut the remaining holes.

3

From the access hole, start cutting on a gentle arc that meets the cutting line and allows you to keep on track easily as you continue the cut.

In **Up Close**, we magnify part of the action so it's easier to see and understand.

Easy, Rider!

So, your scooter's built and painted up just the way you like and you're rarin' to go, right? Well, hold your horses for just a second and think about safety before you scoot off.

◆ Always wear a helmet and elbow and knee pads when riding, just as you would for in-line skating or skateboarding.
◆ If you are under 8 years old, ride only with an adult present.
◆ Never ride at night.
◆ Ride on smooth pavement in traffic-free areas such as school yards and empty parking lots. Many municipalities now prohibit scooters on public streets.
◆ Avoid steep hills, even short ones.
◆ Never attempt to hitch a ride from a passing car, bicycle, or even another scooter.

Sidebar features offer extra information on everything from how to ride a scooter to the history of screws.

Woodworking Tip

Before you reach the end of your cut, have your helper hold the waste piece. Otherwise, it could fall before your cut is complete, splitting the wood.

Woodworking Tip offers practical advice to help you work better and faster. It's like having a pro standing next to you telling you his or her tricks of the trade.

Personalizing Your Swing

A simple coat or two of paint will make your swing look great and help it last longer. But if you want, there are lots of other options you can try. One choice is to stain your seat *(below, left)*. Another possibility is to make a stencil of some design such as a cat's face *(below, right)* and spray-paint it over your base coat. Whatever finish you apply, make sure it's designed for outdoor use.

Sometimes we show you how to make your project a little different by **customizing** it.

Work Safely!

Woodworking can be a lot of fun, so why let an accident spoil a day with your young apprentice? Here are a few tips to help you enjoy this great hobby safely. Keep them in mind as you prepare for and work through a project.

■ Before you start, remove rings and dangling jewelry that might get caught up in a power tool.

■ Keep pets away from your work area.

■ Work in a well-lit space and build your projects on a sturdy work surface.

■ Always wear safety glasses when hammering, drilling, or using a power saw.

■ Follow the manufacturer's instructions for any tools you use.

■ Find a comfortable posture to work. Overreaching or bending improperly can lead to muscle strain and back pain.

■ Always concentrate on what you are doing. If you are tired, put your tools away and try again later when you are well rested.

■ Keep your hands and fingers a safe distance from turning bits and blades on power tools.

■ Keep power tools dry and away from water. Unplug a tool as soon as you've finished using it.

■ Keep all of your tools stored safely out of the reach of children. An enthusiastic youngster might try to get at them without your knowledge.

■ Accidents can happen to even the most cautious of woodworkers. Always keep a fully equipped first-aid kit close at hand when you work.

Let's Get Some Wood

No matter how well it's built, a woodworking project will only be as good as the wood it's made from. Buy the right kind of wood for the project you are making and be picky when it comes time to choose individual boards. You'll be rewarded when you see the finished product.

A World of Wood

All About Wood

The lumber we use for the projects in this book can be classified in one of two categories: softwoods and hardwoods. Most of the projects are built from pine, a softwood that looks good and is not too expensive. It's also easy to cut and shape. Other softwoods include cedar and poplar. Hardwoods are more expensive. Popular species include maple, oak, cherry, and birch. Another type of wood is actually man-made. The most familiar is plywood. It's not cut directly from a tree, but glued together in a factory. Medium-density fiberboard (MDF) is another wood product made from wood chips that are heated, mixed with chemicals, and heat-pressed into panels.

The Size of It

One of the first things you should know about lumber is that a 2-by-4 isn't really 2 inches by 4 inches: It is actually only 1 1/2 inches thick and 3 1/2 inches wide. Lumber is sold according to a board's nominal size in inches—its size before the four sides are planed smooth. The chart below shows nominal and actual dimensions of common lumber sizes.

Nominal Inches		Actual Inches
1 x 1	=	3/4 x 3/4
1 x 2	=	3/4 x 1 1/2
1 x 3	=	3/4 x 2 1/2
1 x 4	=	3/4 x 3 1/2
1 x 6	=	3/4 x 5 1/2
1 x 8	=	3/4 x 7 1/2
1 x 10	=	3/4 x 9 1/2
2 x 2	=	1 1/2 x 1 1/2
2 x 4	=	1 1/2 x 3 1/2
2 x 6	=	1 1/2 x 5 1/2

Did You Know...

A Knot in Wood Was Once a Branch

Ever wonder what makes those hard, dark circles called knots in a piece of wood? Well, the lumber we buy is cut from tree trunks, and knots are simply the part of the trunk where a branch once grew. If the branch was already dead at the time when the tree was cut, the knot might be loose or even have fallen out of the board and left a hole.

Choosing Wood

Examine Every Board

Insect and fire damage, disease, and, most of all, careless drying and storage can make lumber defective. Examine every board carefully before you purchase it.

♦ Peer down the length of a board to see if it is straight *(right)*. Rotate the board to check both faces and edges. You can also lay the board flat on the ground and check it for flatness. Unless the board is straight and flat, don't buy it.

♦ Check the ends of all boards for splits or checks *(see below)*.

Decay-Resistant Woods

Most woods will do just fine outdoors if you protect them well with a few coats of exterior finish. But regardless of how they are protected, some kinds of woods naturally resist decay better than others. That's because of the tannins, oils, and natural resins in the wood.

Cedar and redwood are good choices for outdoor projects. They are highly resistant to decay and not too expensive. Log-cabin builders have traditionally sunk cedar posts in the ground as supports because they are very slow to rot. Farmers used to use cedar, too, for split-rail fences because the rails lasted a long time, no matter what the weather. Others woods, such as teak and walnut, are decay-resistant as well, but cost a lot—especially teak, one of the world's most expensive woods.

What to Look For

Here are some typical defects you can find in wood:

♦ Knots are natural defects—dark, hard circles of wood left behind by a branch *(see opposite Did You Know?)*. They can be extremely tough to saw or nail through. As long as they won't affect your project's strength and as long as you don't care about the appearance—some people actually like the look of knots—you can still use a board with knots as long as they aren't loose. Boards with loose knots are not good. The knots may pop out after your project is assembled.

♦ Warps such as cups, bows, twists, and crooks are usually caused because the wood wasn't dried or stored properly. If you find yourself with a cupped, bowed, twisted, or crooked board, try to save short sections that are good. Some cupped boards can be cut lengthwise to make good narrow boards. Avoid severe warps of any kind.

♦ Checks and splits are narrow breaks at the ends of boards, running in the direction of the wood grain. Don't buy boards with these defects. If you should find them in your boards only later on, cut them off.

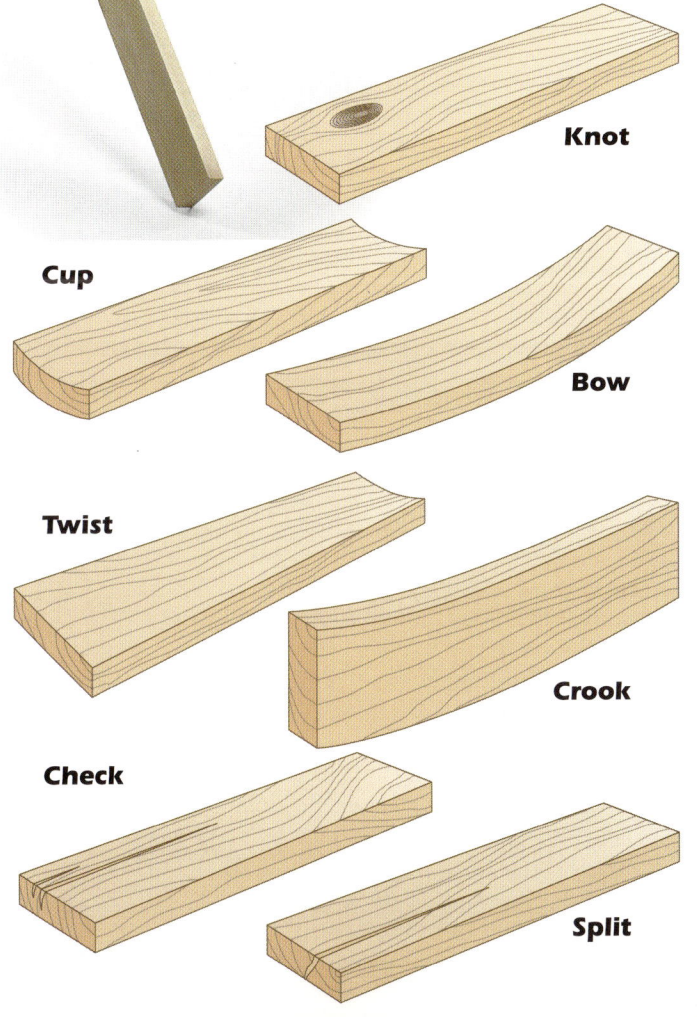

Knot

Cup

Bow

Twist

Crook

Check

Split

Tool Inventory

With these basic measuring and marking, fastening, cutting, and shaping tools, you'll be ready to tackle any of the woodworking projects in this book. Not all of them are classic woodworking tools, but each has its place in the family toolbox. To get a better feel for a tool you aren't familiar with, practice using it on scraps of wood.

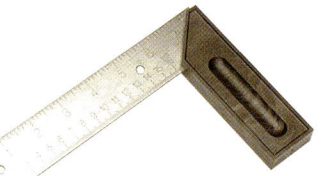

◆ Try square
Checks and marks 90-degree angles. It's great for extending a mark across the face of a board.

◆ Ratchet and socket set
Works like a wrench, but with a cranking motion that speeds up the work of tightening and loosening nuts and hex-head screws. Interchangeable sockets fit a variety of nut and screw-head sizes.

◆ Combination square
Checks and marks 45- and 90-degree angles. Its handle slides along a metal ruler for easy measuring and marking.

◆ Tape measure
A measuring and marking tool, usually with lines every 1/16 inch. Comes in different lengths. A 16-foot model is a good choice for woodworking.

◆ Hammer
Drives nails into wood. Its claw is normally used to pry out poorly driven nails. Available in a range of weights from 12 to 20 ounces.

◆ Carpenter's square
Checks and marks 90-degree angles on large pieces. Can double as a ruler or straightedge.

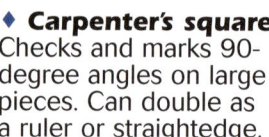

◆ Hand drill
A manual drill, also called an "egg beater." Its handles rotate a pair of gears that turn a drill bit held in a chuck.

◆ Straightedge
A long, flat metal blade. Perfect for marking long, straight lines and checking the flatness of surfaces. A metal ruler can also serve as a shorter straightedge.

◆ Electric drill
For drilling holes and driving screws. Accepts a wide variety of different sized bits. Cordless model offers portability, but usually not the same power as a corded drill.

◆ Screwdrivers
For tightening screws by hand. Available in a number of sizes for screws with slotted, Phillips, and Robertson heads.

◆ Awl
Makes tiny starter holes in wood for screws and nails. Also used instead of a pencil to mark lines in wood.

◆ Adjustable wrenches
Their jaws adjust to fit the heads of a wide range of nuts and hex-head screws. Available in a number of different sizes.

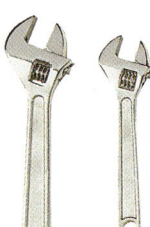

◆ Nail set
Struck with a hammer to sink the protruding heads of finishing nails below the surface of wood.

◆ Compass
A marking tool for drawing arcs and circles.

◆ Tongue-and-groove pliers
Also called slip-jaw or channel-joint pliers. Their adjustable jaws open wide. Although used most often in plumbing, they're great for crimping.

◆ Long-nose pliers
A common electrician's tool, usually used to hook wire. Ridges inside the long, narrow jaws provide a strong grip on nail heads or other hardware.

◆ Wire cutters
A common electrician's tool for snipping wires. Also called cutters, cutting pliers, and lineman's pliers.

◆ Ripsaw
A handsaw designed for cutting wood with the grain (usually along the length of a board).

◆ Crosscut saw
A handsaw with fine teeth designed for cutting wood against the grain (usually across a board).

◆ Plane
An all-purpose wood-shaving tool. Perfect for smoothing, flattening, and shaping wood by hand.

◆ Utility knife
An all-purpose cutting tool with a thin, retractable, and replaceable blade. Can be used to score lines in wood or to cut veneers.

◆ Rasp
A hand tool used for shaping wood. Perfect for rounding over corners.

◆ Sanding block
A rubber or metal block to which a piece of sandpaper is attached to provide a flat sanding surface.

◆ Tin snips
A large, sturdy pair of scissors with sharp tongs for cutting through metal.

◆ Saber saw
An electric, hand-held cutting tool. Its thin blade and easy handling make it ideal for cutting arcs, circles, or other patterns in wood.

◆ Backsaw
A crosscut saw with a reinforced spine. Often used in a miter box to cut miters and other angles in wood.

◆ Clamps
Available in different types and models. Most, like the quick-action trigger clamp (top) and the C clamp (bottom), are ideal for securing a board to a work surface or holding pieces together during assembly.

◆ Wood chisel
For cutting and shaping wood. Can be used with hand pressure alone or tapped with a mallet or hammer.

◆ Caulking gun
A plastic or metal cylinder with a housing for a tube of caulk. When the gun's trigger is squeezed, caulk is forced from the tube's nozzle.

◆ Putty knife
A tool with a flat, flexible metal blade used for filling small nail holes with wood putty. Also useful for scraping off dried glue and other smoothing jobs.

◆ Miter box
A wooden box that works as a guide for cutting angles with a backsaw. Has precut slots to hold the saw blade and cut angles at 45 and 90 degrees. Metal models that adjust to cut any angle are also available.

Seven Things You Should Know

When you consider what some master woodworkers can do with a few pieces of wood, you can understand how starting out might be a little overwhelming for some children. But woodworking isn't rocket science, it's more of an art. And just as a young artist needs to learn a few basic brush strokes, a novice woodworker needs to grasp a few carpentry basics. We call them the "seven things you should know." Teach them well. Works of art will follow...in time.

1. Measuring and Marking

Using a tape measure

Marking a board with a tape measure is easy, but that doesn't mean you shouldn't take the time to do it right. Even though 1/8 inch here or there may not seem like much, especially in rough carpentry, it's enough to mess up even the simplest of woodworking projects.

1

♦ Position the tape about 1/8 inch in from the edge you are marking so you'll have room to make a mark. For an accurate measurement, keep the tape as parallel to the edge as possible.

♦ Line up a sharp pencil with the correct measurement point on the tape and make a small straight mark there on the wood *(right)*.

2

Extending a mark

After you've marked a board for cutting, extend the mark across the face of the piece with a try square. This way you'll have a perfectly straight line to follow when you cut the wood.

♦ Butt the handle of the try square up against one edge of the marked board and line up the outside of the blade with the mark.

♦ Hold the square with one hand and align a sharp pencil over the mark on the board with the other. Pull the pencil down from the mark along the blade of the square *(left)*. Make sure you hold the square perfectly still.

2. Sawing

Starting a handsaw cut

The waste piece is the part of a board that you aren't using after you make a cut. It's a good idea to mark the waste piece with an "X" before cutting, especially if it is close in length to the piece you want to keep.

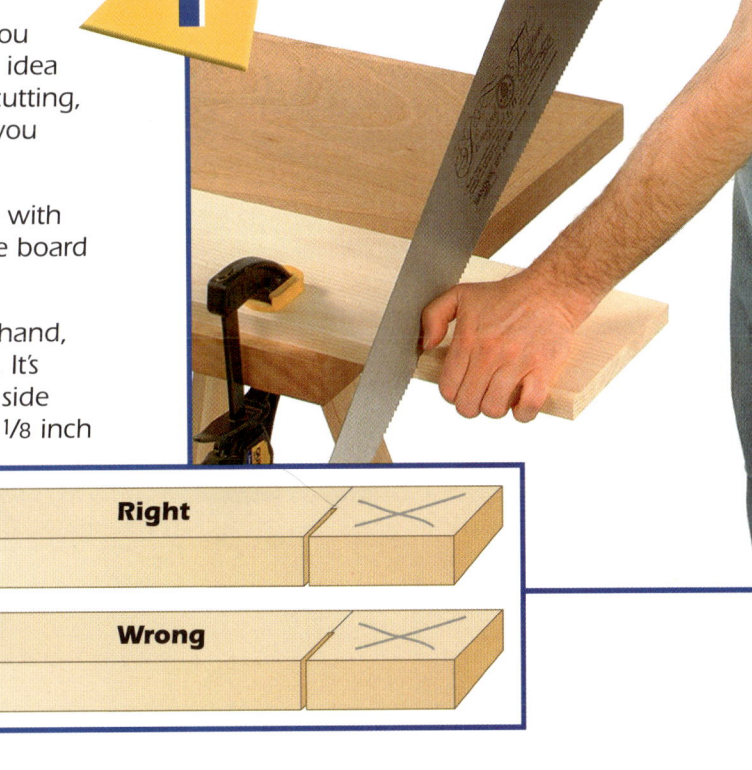

- Clamp the wood to a steady work surface with the cutting line and the shorter part of the board overhanging the table.

- Holding the overhanging piece with one hand, align the saw just outside the cutting line. It's important to make your cut on the waste side of the line. Because saw blades are up to 1/8 inch thick, you'll lose that much of the good piece if you cut directly along the line *(inset)*. With the blade at an angle of about 45 degrees to the board, pull the saw toward you for a few strokes using the thumb of your free hand as a guide *(right)*. This will make a groove, or "kerf," deep enough to hold the saw blade and get the cut started on line.

Right

Wrong

Finishing a handsaw cut

Once your cut is properly started, begin sawing through the piece with steady push-and-pull strokes. For crosscuts (cuts against the grain of the wood—normally cutting a board to length), keep the saw at a 45-degree angle while sawing. For rip cuts (cuts with the grain—normally cutting a board to width), hold the saw at approximately 60 degrees. For a really smooth cut, hold the saw as parallel to the cut line as you can—about 20 degrees.

- Gradually raise the angle of the blade as you saw and support the overhanging piece with your free hand near the end of the cut *(left)*. This will help prevent the cut piece from tearing the clamped piece as it falls away when the cut is complete.

Using a saber saw

3

Although there are handsaws specially made for cutting curves and patterns, it takes a lot of practice to use them well. A power tool called a saber saw can do the same job quickly and easily. It's simple and safe to use.

◆ Clamp your workpiece to a steady work surface with the marked cutting line overhanging the table by a few inches. Line up the blade of the saw with the line. With the base of the saw flat on the workpiece, squeeze the trigger on the saw and slowly feed the blade into the piece *(right)*. Some woodworkers drape the power cord over one shoulder to prevent the cord from being cut accidentally.

◆ When a cutting line curves or turns too sharply to be cut by turning the saw, simply steer the saw off one edge of the workpiece, then stop and attack the cutting line from another angle *(inset)*.

Did You Know...

Sawing Through the Ages

Although the handsaw can be traced back to the early Egyptians or even the Stone Age, we have the innovative Romans to thank for the saws we use today. They were the first to "set" the teeth of a saw so they angle slightly outward from the blade. This creates a cut, or "kerf," slightly wider than the blade itself, which prevents the blade from binding in the wood. The Romans were also the first to start making saw blades from iron. Before them, blades had been made first from stone (too brittle) and later from bronze (too flimsy).

Improvements in ironwork during the Industrial Age made for far more effective saws. Before long, the timber used in the building trades was being cut with two-man crosscut saws (left). A man at each end of a saw that could be 10 feet long would push and pull a blade through a tree until the time came to yell, "Timber!" By the early to mid-20th century, however, gas-powered chain saws had pushed the handsaw out of the forest and into the home workshop, where it does most of its work today.

3. Fastening

Starting a nail

Nailing is simple enough, but take your time and pay attention to your work to avoid crooked nails and sore thumbs. Both can be a real pain. If you are nailing near the end of a board, drill starter holes to prevent the wood from splitting.

♦ Hold the nail at about mid-shaft between your thumb and forefinger. Line it up over a marked nail position or starter hole and hold it as straight as possible. Get it started with two or three taps of a hammer *(right)*. Once the nail is on its way, remove your fingers from it and drive it into the workpiece with a few sharp taps.

Using a nail set

Unlike rough carpentry, woodworking demands invisible nail heads. After they have been driven in flush with the surface of a workpiece, the finishing nails used in woodworking must be driven out of sight with a tool called a nail set.

♦ Place a nail set on the head of the nail, then tap it sharply with a hammer *(left)*. Check that the nail is sufficiently buried by passing a finger over the wood. If you still feel the nail head, repeat the procedure. Then, fill the hole left in the wood with some wood putty and smooth it with a putty knife. Once the putty dries, sand the surface smooth.

Wood Fasteners

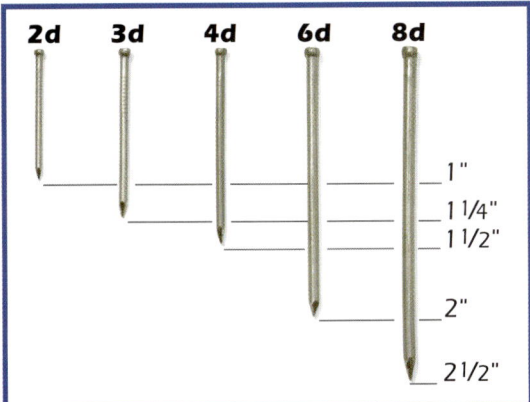

2d	3d	4d	6d	8d

1"
1 1/4"
1 1/2"
2"
2 1/2"

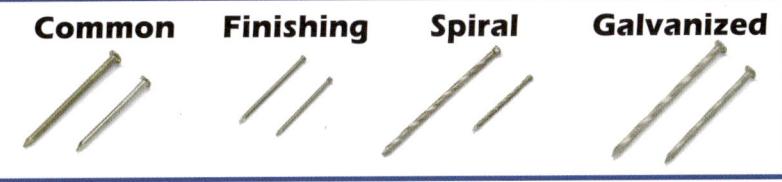

Common   Finishing   Spiral   Galvanized

Nail sizes are often given as "d" or penny (the original price per hundred). The chart at left gives the actual length for some of the most common sizes used in woodworking. A 6d (6-penny) nail is 2 inches long. Nails come in different varieties: Common nails have a large flat head and are used mostly in rough carpentry. Finishing nails are the woodworker's favorite as their small head is easily hidden. Spiral nails provide a strong grip. Galvanized nails are rustproof and intended for outdoor use.

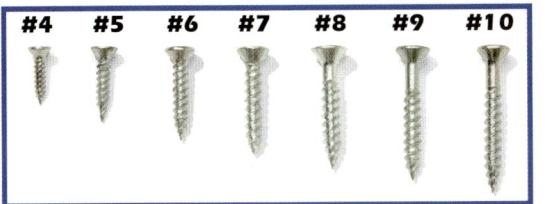

#4	#5	#6	#7	#8	#9	#10

Screw sizes are given in gauge numbers that reflect the diameter of the shank. The higher the number, the thicker the shank—and the stronger the holding power. The most popular sizes of wood screws are shown at left. Each gauge number comes in a range of lengths, with the larger gauges commonly found from 1 1/4 to 4 inches. Woodworking usually requires flat-head screws, although round-head screws are also used when working with thin wood. Oval-head screws may be used for decorative purposes.

4. Drilling

Using a power drill

When you need a hole, whether it's a through hole for a bolt or a starter or pilot hole for a screw or nail, you need an electric drill. It gets the job done quickly and is safe to use if handled correctly.

♦ Most holes are drilled with a twist bit like the one shown in the main illustration here. Clamp the workpiece to a worktable and place the bit on the wood at the location where you want the hole. Slowly squeeze the trigger on the drill. As the bit bites into the wood, squeeze the trigger more firmly and press down on the drill with a little more force. Keep the drill as perpendicular as possible to your workpiece.

♦ When you don't want a hole to go all the way through a piece, you can attach a device called a stop collar to the bit or you can attach what's called a "depth flag." Just measure the depth of hole you need on the bit and attach a strip of masking tape there. Stop drilling when the tape reaches the surface of the workpiece *(right)*. When you do want to drill all the way through, protect your work surface by placing a piece of scrap wood between it and the workpiece.

♦ Among the more useful drill bits for woodworking is the spade bit *(inset)*. It comes in different sizes and can drill a hole up to 1 1/2 inches in diameter. A spade bit is a little trickier to control than a twist bit, especially when the flat part of the blade starts to eat into the wood. So, make sure your workpiece is clamped firmly in place and hold the drill firmly as the spade bit chews through the wood.

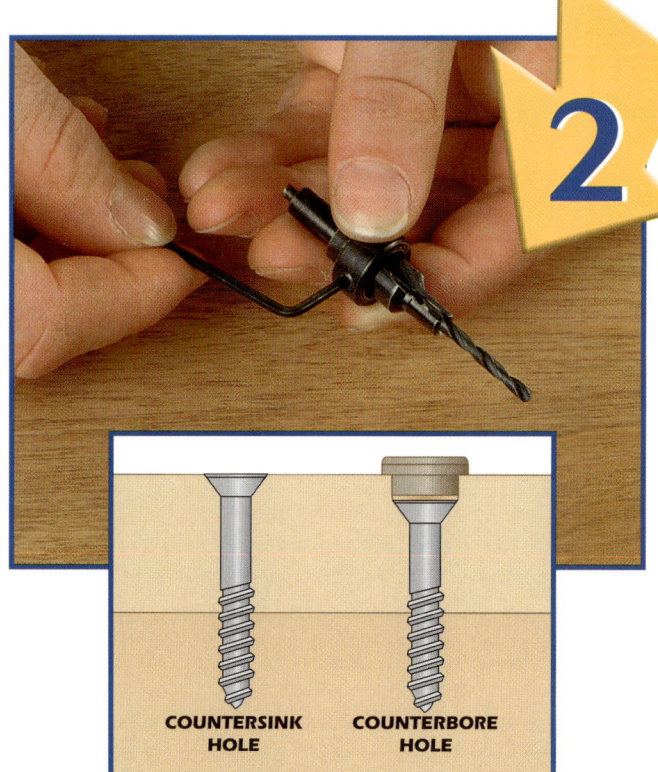

COUNTERSINK HOLE   COUNTERBORE HOLE

Drilling countersink and counterbore holes

In addition to drilling pilot holes for screws (make them a little deeper than half the screw length), a combination bit can widen the top of a hole to enable a screw head to be driven flush with the surface. This is called a countersink hole *(inset, left)*. The bit can also deepen the wide part of the hole so a wood plug can be used to hide the screw. This is a counterbore hole *(inset, right)*.

♦ To drill a countersink hole, tighten a stop collar around the bit about 1/4 inch above the bottom of the wide part of the bit *(left)*. The bit will stop burrowing when the collar touches the wood.

♦ For a counterbore hole, place the collar farther up the bit by an amount equal to the length of the wood plug you'll use to hide the screw. A counterbore hole is also useful when you need to add to the reach of a screw. By counterboring a hole 1 inch deep, for example, a 2 1/2-inch screw will pass through a 3 1/2-inch piece of wood.

5. Gluing

Spreading glue

Woodworkers often use wood glue, such as yellow carpenter's glue, as well as nails and screws to fasten wood to wood. Glue adds strength to the overall assembly and creates a continuous bond between the pieces.

♦ Squeeze a thin bead of glue down the middle of the edge of the workpiece you want to glue up. Be careful to use the right amount of glue—just enough to spread a thin layer on the surface. Too little glue and you won't get the desired bond; too much will make a mess of your project.

♦ Spread the glue evenly with a wooden popsicle stick or stir stick *(right)*. Assemble your pieces quickly before the glue has time to dry. Wipe off any excess glue with a damp cloth.

6. Clamping

Using clamps

Having clamps around is like having an extra pair of strong hands. No workshop is complete without them. Although they come in a number of different models and sizes, including specialty types, the quick-action trigger type shown here is relatively inexpensive, versatile, and easy to use. The jaws are covered with rubber pads to protect the workpiece from dents and scratches.

♦ Use clamps to secure a workpiece for cutting or drilling *(left, top)* or to help hold wood pieces together during assembly *(left, bottom)*.

♦ C clamps are another useful type of clamp to have around. Their smaller jaws come in handy when you have a narrow surface to clamp *(inset)*. Remember to place small pieces of scrap wood between the clamp jaws and the workpiece so you don't leave marks in the wood.

7. Sanding

Sanding by hand

No matter how well you build a project, its appearance often depends on how well it is sanded.

♦ To sand a small area by hand, load a sanding block with the appropriate grit of sandpaper. Remove bumps, scratches, and other imperfections with coarse (40- to 60-grit) paper. Use medium (80- to 120-grit) paper to smooth flat surfaces and sharp edges. Make a final pass before painting or staining with fine (150- to 180-grit) paper.

♦ Smooth over sharp edges by sanding with the block at a 45-degree angle *(right)*. Sand flat areas with long, fluid strokes. Always sand with the grain of the wood, not against it.

Using a palm sander

For large surfaces that would take too long to sand by hand, use a palm sander.

♦ Load the sander with the appropriate grit of sandpaper *(step 1)*.

♦ If necessary, clamp the piece you want to sand to a steady work surface. Turn on the sander and gently bring it down to the wood surface. Keep the tool moving forward at all times *(left)*. Never stop it in one spot. When you reach the end of a pass, bring the sander back and slightly overlap your first pass. Keep working this way until you've sanded the entire surface.

Woodworking Tip

Here's a trick to help you get the most out of a sheet of sandpaper when sanding by hand. Fold a sheet of sandpaper into quarters, then unfold it and cut it halfway down one fold (below, left). Now you can fold the paper so that no two abrasive sides touch each other (below; center, right). Use the sheet like a sanding pad. When one side wears out, refold the sheet to uncover a fresh abrasive side.

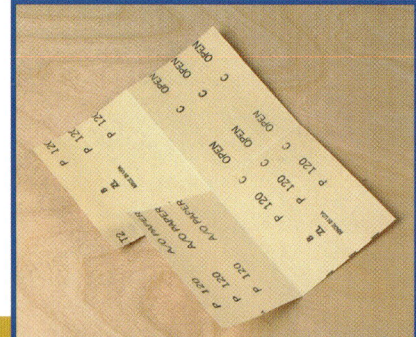

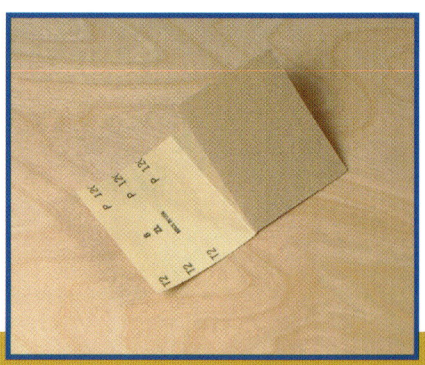

Chapter 1
Making Your Own Fun

Push Scooter

Here's a project to really get you going! This scooter is fun to build, and when you're finished, all you'll need to add is a push with your foot.

Scooters usually have only two wheels like bicycles, but our model uses two sets of skateboard wheels, which provide greater stability than standard wheels. And they're easy to attach! The upright supporting the handle is tapered and rounded to give the scooter a cool, aerodynamic look, while the sturdy plywood base is the perfect platform for 6- to 10-year-old movers and shakers!

Materials you'll need

Wood	30 inches x 9 inches 3/4-inch plywood 2 feet 1x4 pine 1 foot 1x3 pine 1 foot 1-inch dowel
Hardware	2 2¾-inch x 2-inch right-angle brackets
Fasteners	#8 1½-inch screws #10 ¾-inch round-head screws 1½-inch round-head bolts and lock nuts
Miscellaneous	Wood glue 2 sets skateboard wheels (new or from an old skateboard)

The tools you'll need...

Try square

Electric drill with 1-inch spade bit, 3/32- and 3/16-inch twist bits, #8 combination bit, and screwdriver bit.

Straightedge

Tape measure

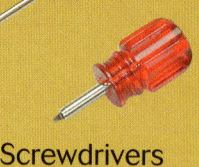

Screwdrivers

How the pieces fit together...

♦ The front and back wheel sets, or "trucks," are centered between the edges of the base. They're fastened with bolts and lock nuts through holes drilled into the base.

♦ The tapered upright is attached to the base with two metal brackets. A wood brace fastened to both the base and the front edge of the upright adds stability.

♦ The dowel handle fits in a hole drilled at the top of the upright and is held with wood glue and a screw.

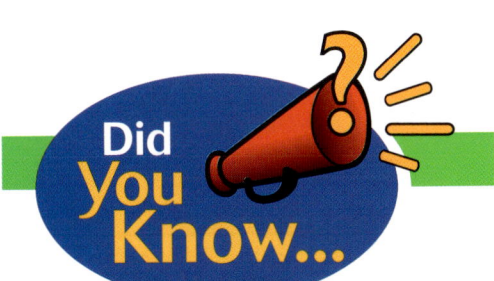

Did You Know...

How to Ride a Scooter

Put one foot on the scooter—not too close to the front—making sure your toes are pointing forward. Keep most of your weight on this foot. Now, push off with the other foot, keeping both hands on the handle. And don't forget to check out our safety tips, "Easy, Rider!," on page 29 at the end of this project.

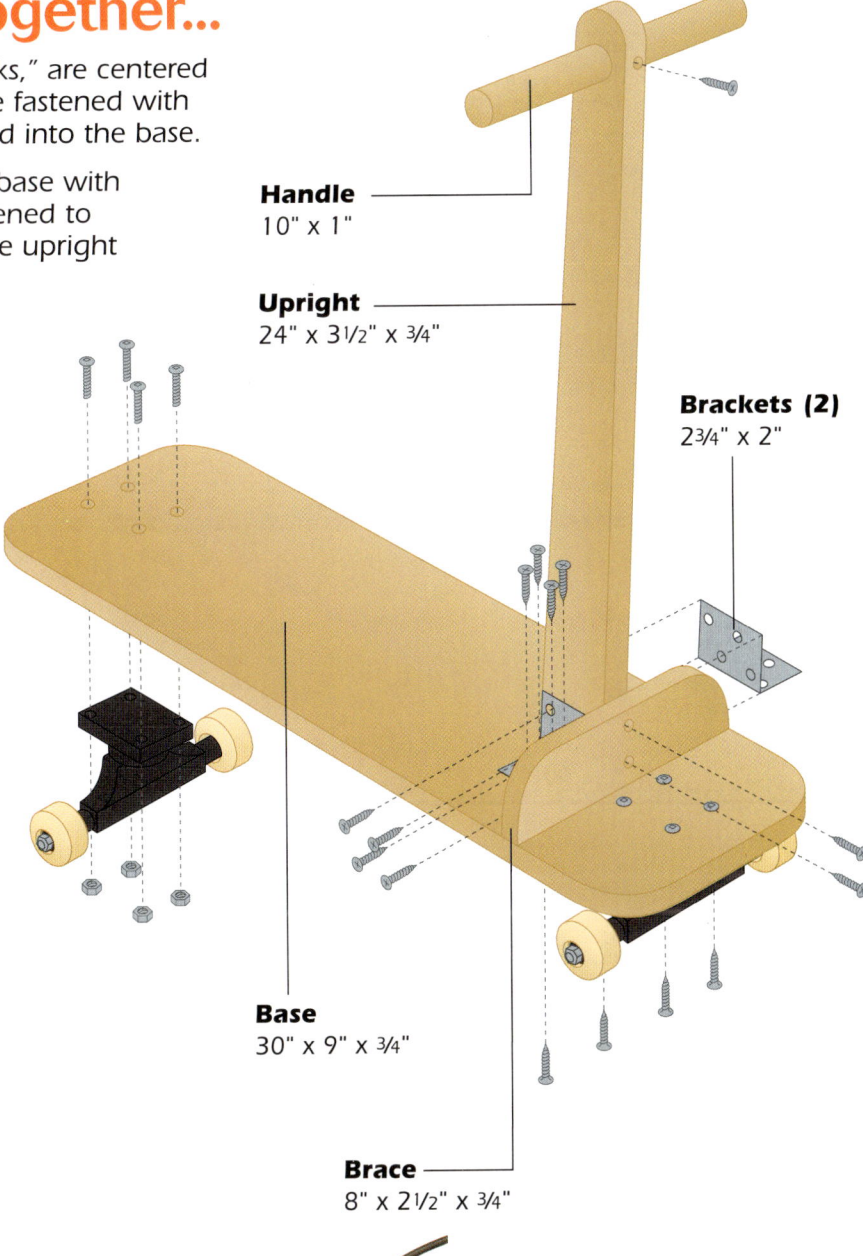

Handle
10" x 1"

Upright
24" x 3½" x ¾"

Brackets (2)
2¾" x 2"

Base
30" x 9" x ¾"

Brace
8" x 2½" x ¾"

Adjustable wrench

Compass

Sanding block and 120-grit sandpaper

Saber saw

Clamps

Marking round corners on the base

1

♦ Cut all the pieces of the scooter to size.

♦ At one corner of the base, mark two lines 2 inches in from the side and end.

♦ Adjust a compass to scribe a circle with a radius of 2 inches and place the point of the compass at the point where the lines meet. Draw an arc that touches the side and end of the board *(right)*.

♦ Repeat at the other three corners.

Curving the corners

A saber saw is the best tool for cutting round corners of this size.

2

♦ Clamp the base to your worktable with one end extending beyond the table's edge. Use two clamps to make sure the piece is secure.

♦ Turn on the saw and ease the blade into the workpiece at one of the curved pencil marks. Follow the mark, cutting slowly to avoid straying off line *(left)*.

♦ Cut the second corner, then reposition the workpiece to cut the other two corners.

♦ Sand all the surfaces of the base with 120-grit sandpaper.

Tapering the upright

♦ Measure and mark a point on the edge of the upright 2 inches from one end.

♦ At the opposite end of the upright, measure and mark a point 1½ inches from the edge.

♦ Connect the two points with a straightedge *(right)*.

3

4

Before you reach the end of your cut, have your helper hold the waste piece. Otherwise, it could fall before your cut is complete, splitting the wood.

Cutting the taper

♦ Clamp the upright to the worktable so the marked edge extends beyond the edge of the table.

♦ With a saber saw, trim the upright along the taper line, starting at the 1 1/2-inch mark *(left)*.

Rounding the corners of the upright

The upper end of the upright is rounded to match the corners of the base. You can round with a rasp or your saber saw.

♦ Lay the upright on the worktable. Scribe an arc at the top end of the upright with a compass. Or, use a soup can to make the mark, lining up the rim of the can with the edges of the upright.

♦ Clamp the upright to the table, extending the marked corners past the table's edge.

♦ Cut along your mark with a saber saw *(right)*.

♦ Finish the job with a sanding block fitted with 120-grit sandpaper. Then, smooth the other surfaces of the upright.

5

Up Close...

Cutting the hole for the handle

- Clamp the upright to the table with a scrap piece underneath to protect the table.

- Measure and mark a point on the face of the upright 1 1/2 inches down from the top of the rounded end. Center the point between the edges.

- Fit a drill with a 1-inch spade bit, then drill straight down through the upright at the marked center point *(right)*.

6

When you need a hole bigger than any regular drill bit can make (more than $3/8$ inch), use a spade bit. These flat bits with sharp, pointed tips are sized to drill holes up to $1^1/2$ inches in diameter. Find and mark the center of the hole you want to drill. To make drilling a little easier, drill a small starter hole or punch one with an awl at the center mark to help get the bit started on line.

Marking the bracket screw holes

- Hold one of the brackets flat against the upright so the taller flange of the bracket is centered between the edges of the upright and the shorter flange is even with the bottom end.

- Mark the position of the bracket screw holes on the upright *(left)*.

- Turn over the upright and mark the bracket screw holes on its other side.

7

8

Fastening the brackets to the upright

♦ Clamp the upright, then fit your drill with a 3/32-inch bit. Wrap a strip of masking tape around the bit 1 inch from the tip as a depth flag and drill a pilot hole at each mark on the upright.

♦ Reposition one of the brackets on the upright and fasten it in place, driving 3/4-inch round-head screws into the drilled holes.

♦ Attach the other bracket to the upright *(left)*.

9

Positioning the upright on the base

To make your scooter well balanced, it's important to center the upright between the edges of the base.

♦ Lay the base face up on the worktable. Measure and mark a point 4 3/4 inches from the front end.

♦ Draw a pencil line straight across the surface of the base at the point, using a try square to make the line perpendicular to the edges.

♦ Measure and mark the midpoint of the line *(right)*. This will be your reference point for positioning the upright and the brace.

10 Marking the bracket holes on the base

♦ Position the upright on the base with the tapered edge facing the back of the scooter. Align the straight edge of the upright with the marked line and the center of the edge with the reference point.

♦ Mark the empty screw holes of both brackets on the base (left).

♦ Set the upright aside for now, then clamp the base to the worktable.

♦ Fit a drill with a 3/32-inch bit and drill a pilot hole for a round-head screw at each mark on the base.

Fastening the upright to the base

♦ Reposition the upright on the base, lining up the bracket screw holes with the pilot holes.

♦ Fasten both brackets to the base, driving round-head screws into the drilled holes (right).

11

12

Preparing the brace

The brace helps to reinforce the upright. It is attached to both the upright and the base.

♦ With a compass set to make a circle with a 2-inch radius, scribe an arc at the two top corners of the brace, as you did for the base in step 1.

♦ Clamp the brace to the edge of the table, then round off the corners with a saber saw. Smooth the corners and edges with a sanding block.

♦ Measure and mark the center of the bottom edge of the brace. Use a try square to extend the center line up the face of the brace (left).

♦ Make two marks on the line 1 1/2 inches from the top and bottom ends.

13

Fastening the brace to the upright

- Set the base on your worktable and lay the brace flush against the front edge of the upright. Line up the center line on the brace with the reference point you marked on the base in step 9, then clamp the brace to the base.

- Fit a drill with a combination bit, adjust the depth to 1 inch, then drill countersink holes through the brace into the upright at each mark on the brace.

- Fasten the brace to the upright through the drilled holes with 1 1/2-inch screws *(right)*.

14

Fastening the brace to the base

- Undo the clamps holding the base and brace together. Set the base upside down on the table with the upright extending off the edge and clamp the base to the table.

- Measure and mark a point 4 3/8 inches from the front end of the base. With a try square, draw a line at the mark across the base.

- Mark four points along the line spaced 1 1/2 inches from each edge and 1 1/2 inches apart.

- Use the drill and combination bit to drill a countersink hole for 1 1/2-inch screws at each mark through the base into the brace.

- Drive a screw into each drilled hole *(left)*.

Positioning the wheel trucks

The wheel trucks at each end of the base are centered between the edges.

15

◆ With the base still upside down, measure and mark center points at its front and back ends. Using a try square, mark a center line from each point a few inches along the underside of the base.

◆ Use the square to make two more lines perpendicular to the center lines offset by 3/4 inch from the front and back ends.

◆ Holding a wheel truck on the base so its front edge aligns with one of the offset lines and the center line divides the truck in half, mark its bolt holes on the base *(right)*.

◆ Mark the bolt holes of the second wheel truck at the other end of the base the same way.

16

Drilling the bolt holes

◆ Clamp the base to the worktable so the marked points at one end overhang the edge.

◆ Fit a drill with a 3/16-inch bit and drill a hole through the base at each mark *(left)*.

◆ Reposition the base and drill the holes at the opposite end.

17

Fastening the wheel trucks to the base

Because most skateboard bases are only 1/2 inch thick, the fasteners that held your wheel trucks in place may not be long enough for the 3/4-inch base of our scooter. You'll need bolts 1 1/2 inches long.

- With the base still clamped upside down, position a wheel truck on it, lining up the truck's bolt holes with the drilled holes in the base.

- Slip the bolts up through the holes one at a time, tightening the lock nuts on the ends as far as they go with your fingers.

- With a helper holding the bolt stationary from underneath with a screwdriver, tighten the nuts with an adjustable wrench *(left, above)*.

- Fasten the other wheel truck to the base.

18

Installing the handle

- Set the scooter on its wheels and spread some wood glue on the inside of the handle hole in the upright. Slide the handle into the hole, centering it in the upright.

- Make a mark on the front edge of the upright, centered on the handle.

- Fit your drill with a combination bit. Then, with a helper holding the handle in position, drill a countersink hole for a 1 1/2-inch screw through the upright into the dowel.

- Drive a screw through the hole into the handle *(above)*.

Easy, Rider!

So, your scooter's built and painted up just the way you like and you're rarin' to go, right? Well, hold your horses for just a second and think about safety before you scoot off.

- Always wear a helmet and elbow and knee pads when riding, just as you would for in-line skating or skateboarding.
- If you are under 8 years old, ride only with an adult present.
- Never ride at night.
- Ride on smooth pavement in traffic-free areas such as school yards and empty parking lots. Many municipalities now prohibit scooters on public streets.
- Avoid steep hills, even short ones.
- Never attempt to hitch a ride from a passing car, bicycle, or even another scooter.

Building a Beanbag Board

Feeling full of beans? Then, this is the project for you.

Little kids will enjoy just trying to toss a bag through one of the holes. Bigger brothers and sisters will want a pad of paper to keep score. You can saw the pieces for the board yourself from a half sheet of plywood, but it's a lot easier to have it cut for you at your local lumberyard. Once you're finished building, you'll probably want to paint the board. You can keep it as simple as a single color with different scores marked under each hole (50, 100, 200, 300, and 500). Or, you can dress it up with something like the clown face on the board here. It's all up to you!

Materials you'll need

Wood	2 24 inches x 36 inches 3/4-inch plywood
Hardware	2 2-inch x 3-inch door hinges

The tools you'll need...

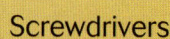
Screwdrivers

Try square

Clamps

Tape measure

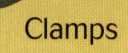
Straightedge

How the pieces fit together...

♦ The front and back panels are ¾-inch plywood panels joined at the top with two door hinges.

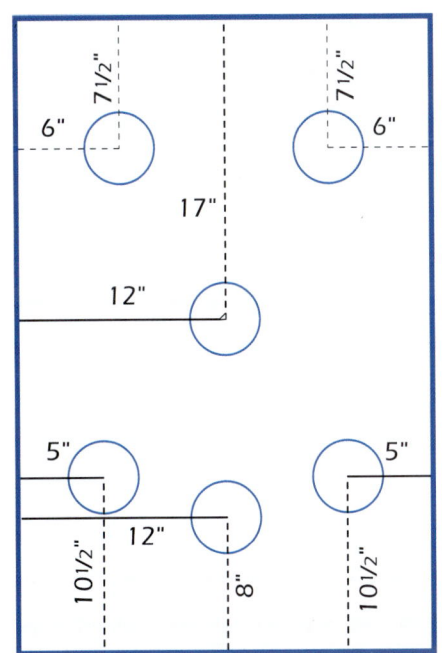

7½" 7½"

6" 6"

17"

12"

5" 5"

10½" 12" 8" 10½"

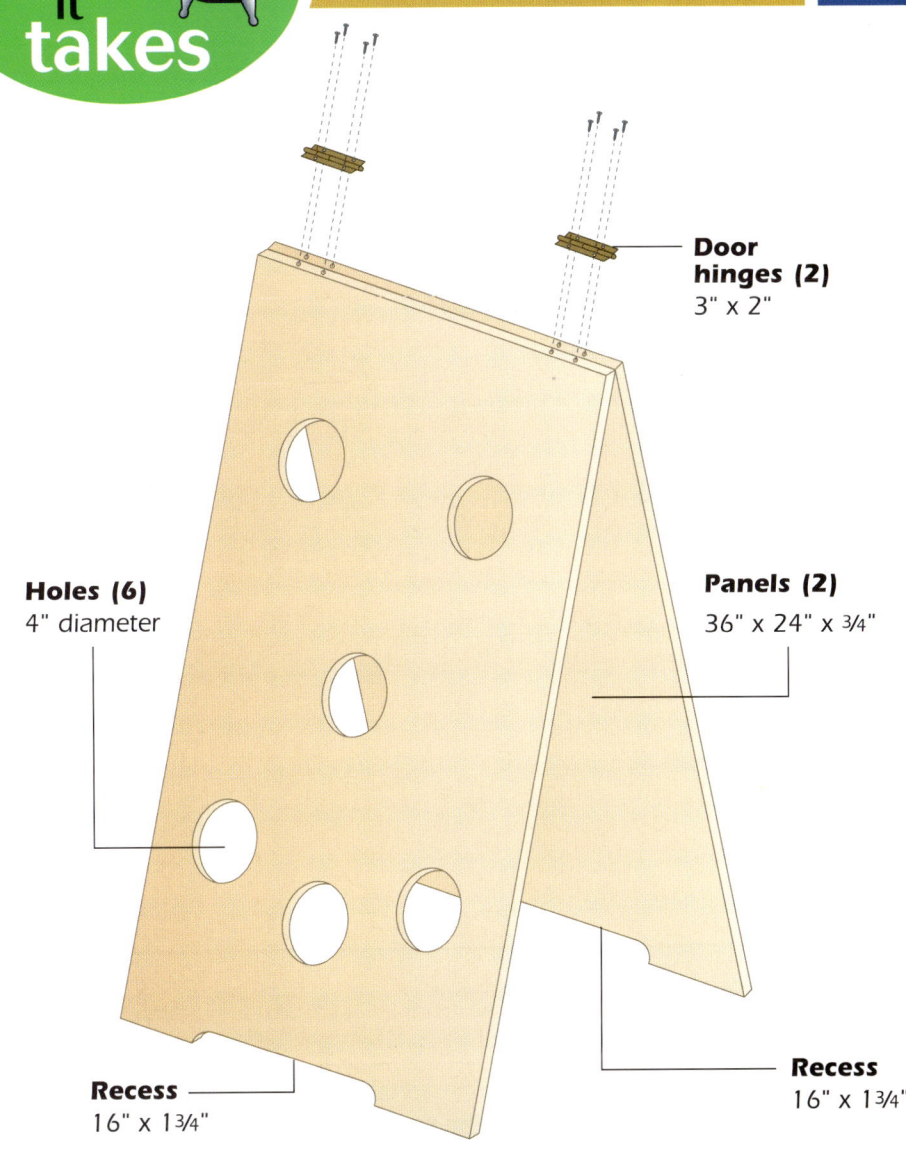

Door hinges (2)
3" x 2"

Panels (2)
36" x 24" x ¾"

Holes (6)
4" diameter

Recess
16" x 1¾"

Recess
16" x 1¾"

Did You Know...

How to Make Your Own Beanbags

You can buy beanbags for your game at a hobby store. Better yet, make your own. Cut two 6-inch squares of heavy-duty fabric and lay the pieces one on top of the other. Sew three sides and halfway along the fourth. Turn the bag inside out and fill it three-quarters full with dried beans (or peas) or sand. Now, finish sewing the last side. If you want something that's even faster to make, find a spare sock, fill the foot end with beans, and tie a knot in the open end.

Saber saw

Sanding block and 120-grit sandpaper

Compass

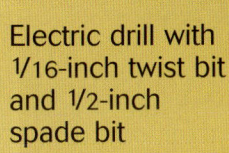

Electric drill with ¹⁄₁₆-inch twist bit and ½-inch spade bit

Marking the beanbag holes

Beanbag holes should be 4 inches in diameter.

♦ The first thing you'll need to do is to figure out where to cut the holes on the front panel. The diagram on page 31 will help you locate them. Measure from the edges of the panel and mark crossing vertical and horizontal lines following the measurements provided. The centers of the holes will be where the lines cross.

♦ Fit a compass with a pencil and adjust the compass to draw a circle with a 2-inch radius. Place the compass point on each marked hole center and draw the circles one at a time *(right)*.

1

2

Drilling access holes

A 4-inch hole is too big to make with a drill. You'll need to use a saber saw instead. But first you'll have to drill an access hole to get the saw blade started on the cut.

♦ Clamp the front panel to your worktable with a piece of scrap wood between it and the table. (You don't want to drill right through into the table!)

♦ Fit your power drill with a 1/2-inch spade bit and drill an access hole through the panel just inside the rim of each circle *(left)*.

Cutting the beanbag holes

- Clamp the front panel to the table with two of the holes overhanging the edge of the table. Fit the blade of a saber saw into an access hole and cut toward the marked line *(right)*.

- Cut halfway around the circle, guiding the saw slowly and carefully to keep the blade on line. Stop the saw, then reposition yourself to make it more comfortable to finish making the cut. Or, you can cut halfway around the circle then complete the cut by sawing in the opposite direction from the access hole.

- Cut the second hole, then shift and reclamp the board to cut the remaining holes.

3

From the access hole, start cutting on a gentle arc that meets the cutting line and allows you to keep on track easily as you continue the cut.

Marking the recesses

4

- Mark a horizontal line across the front panel 1¾ inches from the bottom end. Then, with a try square, make a vertical line 4 inches from each edge, forming a rectangular outline *(left)*. Be sure you keep the arm of the blade flush against the end of the panel while you draw your lines. Draw an identical outline on the back panel.

5

Marking the curve of the recesses

The recesses at the bottom of the panels are curved at each end. The slope of the curve is up to you, but a standard soup can creates an attractive look.

♦ Hold a soup can at one corner of the outline you marked on the front panel in step 4. Position the can so its rim touches both the horizontal and vertical lines. Trace the rim of the can to mark the curve of the recess *(left)*. Repeat on the back panel.

6

Cutting the recesses

♦ Clamp the front panel to the table so the bottom end overhangs the edge of the table.

♦ Align the blade of the saber saw with one end of the cutting line and feed the blade slowly into the panel *(right)*. If the blade starts to bind, stop cutting and finish the cut from the other end. Cut the recess on the back panel.

♦ Once both recesses are cut, sand all the edges of the panels with 120-grit sandpaper.

7 Marking the hinges

This unit is held together by a pair of door hinges screwed to both panels.

◆ Lay the two panels on the worktable top-end to top-end and edges aligned. If one side of the panels is smoother than the other, set them with the good side face down. Leave a 1/4-inch gap between the panels for the hinge pin.

◆ Set one hinge 1 inch from the edges of the panels with its pin centered between them and the leaves flat on them. Outline the leaves on the panels, then mark the screw holes *(left)*. Mark the other hinge at the opposite edges.

Drilling pilot holes for the hinge screws

Pilot holes make it easier to drive the hinge screws and help keep the board from splitting as the screws are driven.

◆ Install a 1/16-inch bit in an electric drill and mark a depth of 5/8 inch on the bit with masking tape.

◆ Line up the bit with one of the screw-hole marks and drill the hole, stopping when the tape just touches the panel *(right)*. Drill the other holes.

8

9

Fastening the hinges to the panels

◆ Hold the hinges within the outline you marked in step 7 and fasten them to the panels with the screws supplied *(left)*.

◆ Once both hinges are in place, your beanbag board is ready to paint. When the paint is dry, start tossing!

Building a Toolbox

The first thing any budding woodworker needs is a good toolbox. The model built here is a good project for kids as young as 8 years old. All it requires is some simple cutting, nailing, and fastening.

This toolbox has ample space for a young woodworker's growing collection of tools. The tool racks are good for holding screwdrivers and pliers, and the strap makes carrying easy. Solidly built, the toolbox should last until well after your little builder is all grown up.

Materials you'll need

Wood	4 feet 1x10 pine
	3 feet 1x6 pine
	3 feet 1x3 pine
Fasteners	1½-inch finishing nails
	#6 1½-inch screws
	#6 ¾-inch screws and washers
Miscellaneous	2 feet 1¼-inch-wide, ¼-inch-thick leather
	Wood glue

The tools you'll need...

Tape measure

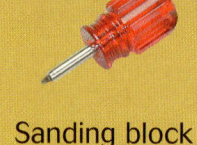
Sanding block and 120-grit sandpaper

Screwdrivers

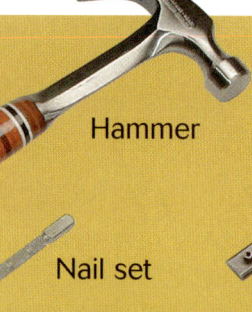
Hammer

Nail set

Clamps

The time it takes

2 hours to build
1 hour to paint

How the pieces fit together...

- The ends of the box are fastened to the sides with finishing nails. The tool racks are nailed to the top of the sides.
- The bottom is screwed to the sides and ends from below.
- Wood glue reinforces all the connections.
- The leather strap handle is screwed to the ends.

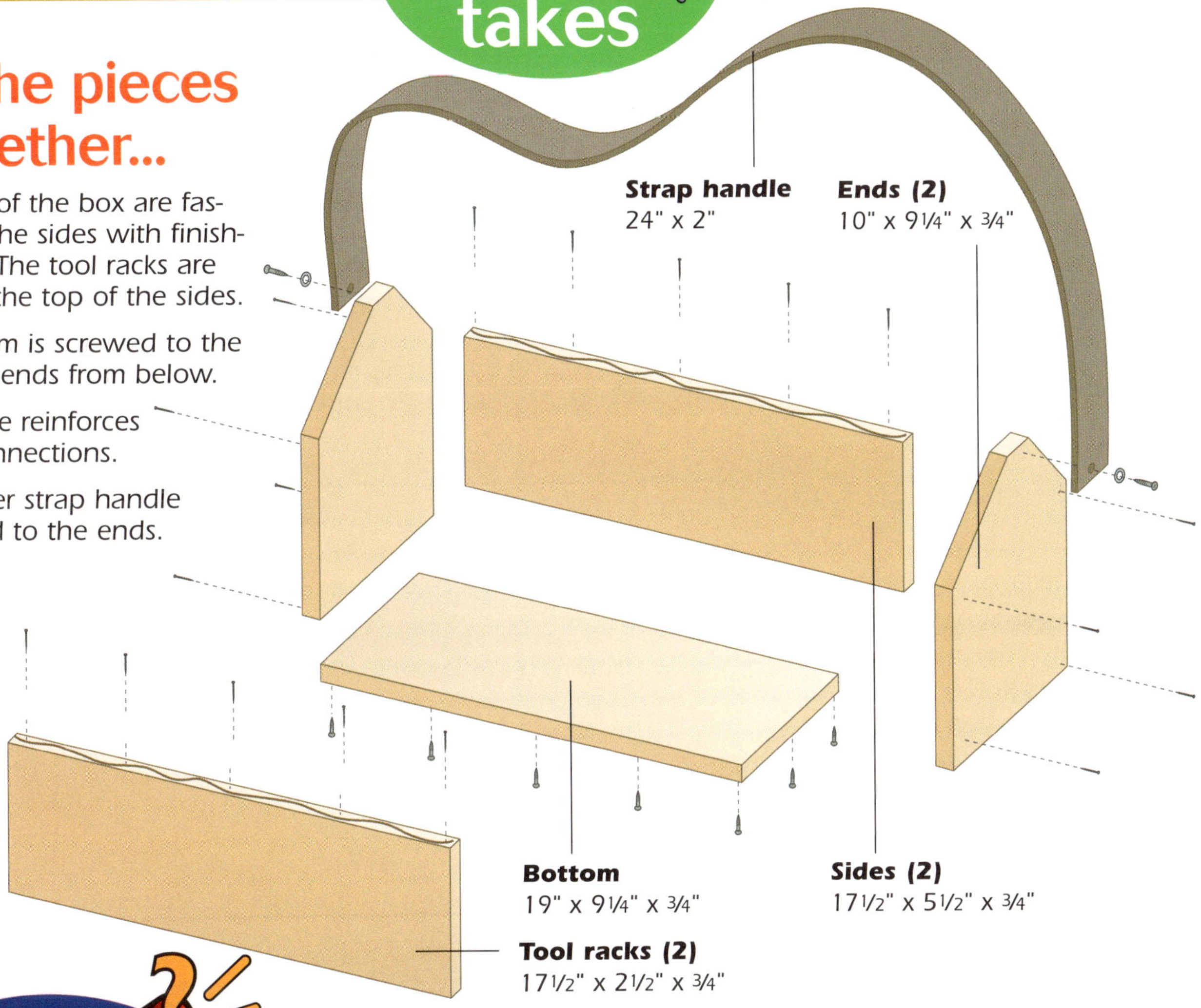
Strap handle
24" x 2"
Ends (2)
10" x 9 1/4" x 3/4"
Bottom
19" x 9 1/4" x 3/4"
Sides (2)
17 1/2" x 5 1/2" x 3/4"
Tool racks (2)
17 1/2" x 2 1/2" x 3/4"

Did You Know...

The Ultimate Toolbox

Toolboxes are handy places to store tools. But they also can be works of art. Just look at the one made by Henry Studley more than 100 years ago in Massachusetts (right). His toolbox, made of fancy woods such as mahogany and ebony, can hold 300 tools—but measures only 39 inches high by 18 inches wide by 9 inches deep!

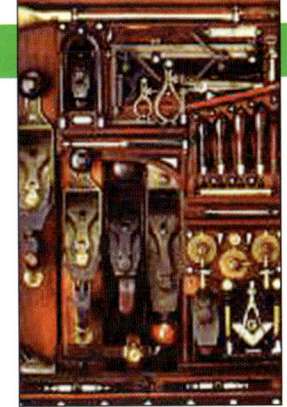

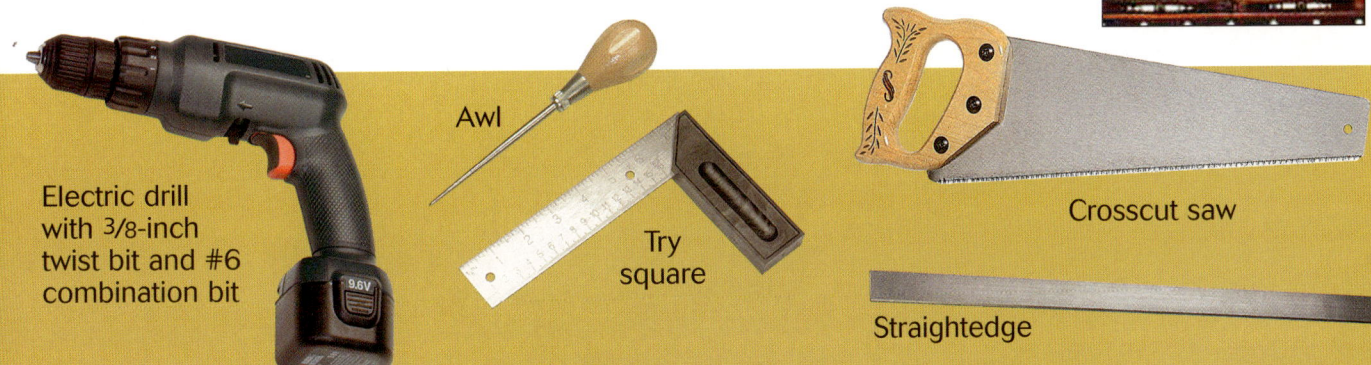

Electric drill
with 3/8-inch
twist bit and #6
combination bit
9.6V
Awl
Try
square
Crosscut saw
Straightedge

1 Marking the taper on the ends

◆ Cut all the pieces of the toolbox to length.

◆ Measure from the top end of one of the end pieces and make a mark 3¼ inches down along each edge. Then, measure 3¾ inches from both edges along the top of the board and make marks there. Connect the marks diagonally with a straightedge *(left)*.

◆ Mark the other end piece the same way.

2 Cutting the tapers

◆ Clamp one end piece to your worktable with one of the cutting lines a few inches clear of the table. Cut along the line with a crosscut saw. Cut the other side of the board, then taper the other end piece the same way *(right)*.

3

Marking the holes in the tool racks

The tool racks feature holes at 2-inch intervals.

◆ Lay the tool racks face down on your worktable. At each end of one of the racks, mark a point 3/8 inch from one edge. Connect the marks with a straightedge. Mark the second tool rack the same way.

◆ Make a mark every 2 inches along the line on one tool rack. Lay out the holes on the second rack *(left)*.

4

Drilling the holes

◆ Clamp one of the racks to the worktable with a piece of scrap wood between it and the table.

◆ Fit your power drill with a 3/8-inch bit and drill a hole through the rack at each of the marks you made in step 3 *(right)*. Drill the holes in the second rack.

Assembling the sides and one end

5

- Mark guidelines along the outside faces of both end pieces 3/8 inch from each edge. Then, make two pencil marks along each line 1 inch from each end. You will drive a nail through the end and into a side piece at each mark.

- Apply a thin bead of wood glue along one end of one side piece, then set the other end flat on the floor. Position an end piece on the side so the edge of the end piece is flush with the outside face of the side. The bottom of the end piece should be flush with the bottom edge of the side. Fasten the boards together by driving nails at the marks, then glue and nail the opposite side in place *(right)*.

6

Woodworking Tip

To prevent a nail from splitting the wood, you can always drill a small pilot hole first. An even quicker way to avoid splitting is to blunt the tip of the nail you will use with a sharp blow from a hammer.

Adding the other end

- With both sides attached to one end, glue and nail the other end to the sides, driving nails at the marks as in step 5. Then, set all the nail heads below the surface: Hold a nail set on each nail head in turn and strike the nail set with the hammer *(left)*.

7

Anchoring the bottom

The bottom is fastened to the ends and sides from underneath with 1½-inch screws.

◆ Before you drive the screws, you'll need to drill countersink holes. Mark a guideline around the outside face of the bottom 3/8 inch from each edge and end. Then, make three evenly spaced pencil marks along each line. You will drive a screw through the bottom and into a side or end piece at each mark and at each corner where the lines cross.

◆ Set the toolbox on one side on the worktable, spread glue on the bottom of the sides and ends, and clamp the bottom in place so its edges and ends are flush with the outside of the box. Install a combination bit in your drill and drill a countersink hole for a screw into the bottom at each mark *(above)*.

◆ Fasten the bottom in place by driving a screw into each hole.

8

Attaching the tool racks

◆ Mark a guideline down the face of both tool racks 3/8 inch from the edge furthest from the holes. Then, make three evenly spaced pencil marks along each line.

◆ Spread some glue along the top edge of a side piece, position one of the tool racks on the side so its outside edge is flush with the outside of the box, and clamp the rack in place. Drive a nail into the rack at each mark and at each end of the rack to fasten it in place *(above)*. Glue and nail the second tool rack to the other side piece.

9

Fastening the strap handle

The handle is made from a 24-inch-long strip of leather 1¼ inches wide and ¼ inch thick. An old belt may fit the bill, or you may have to visit a specialty shop to have a strip of leather cut.

◆ Secure the strap to the worktable on top of a scrap piece of wood and press the point of an awl through the strap 1 inch from each end.

◆ Measure and mark the center of the toolbox end pieces about 1 inch from the top and score the mark with the awl. Slide a 3/4-inch screw with a washer through one hole in the strap and drive it into the end piece with a screwdriver. Repeat to fasten the strap to the other end *(left)*.

Building a Red Wagon

Even if you decide not to paint it red, this wagon is a classic that will last for years. Perfect for the younger set to use as a mini moving van, the red wagon is practical and fun.

The sides are angled and the corners are rounded to give the wagon its classic style. The side rails have the same look as the sides, and they keep your cargo from falling overboard. Swivel wheels at the front and a long handle attached to a sturdy support make pulling this baby a cinch.

Materials you'll need

Wood	22 1/8 inches x 16 inches 3/4-inch plywood
	8 feet 1x6 pine
	4 feet 1x4 pine
	3 feet 1x2 pine
	2 feet 1x1 pine
	2 feet 1-inch dowel
Hardware	4 4-inch plate-type casters (2 standard, 2 swivel) with carriage bolts, washers, and hex nuts
Fasteners	#8 1 1/4-inch screws
	#8 1 1/2-inch screws
	2 2-inch screw eyes
Miscellaneous	Wood glue

The tools you'll need...

Screwdrivers

Try square

Tape measure

Sanding block and 120-grit sandpaper

Electric drill with 1/16-inch, 3/16-inch, and 3/8-inch twist bits and #8 combination bit

Straightedge

How the pieces fit together...

- ♦ The sides, back, and front of the wagon are fastened together with wood glue and screws.

- ♦ The bottom is screwed to the sides, front, and back and is supported by two cleats.

- ♦ The side and back rails are attached to four uprights, which in turn are fastened to the sides and back.

- ♦ The four casters are anchored to the bottom with carriage bolts.

- ♦ The handle is joined to the handle support with interlocking screw eyes. The support is fastened to the front of the wagon with glue and screws.

Back
16" x 5½" x ¾"

Bottom
22⅛" x 16" x ¾"

Back rail
16" x 3½" x ¾"

Uprights (4)
8¼" x 1½" x ¾"

Side rails (2)
12" x 3½" x ¾"

Sides (2)
29¾" x 5½" x ¾"

Handle
24" x 1"

Hand grip
4¼" x 1½" x ¾"

Handle support
5" x 3½" x ¾"

Front
16" x 5½" x ¾"

Cleats
10" x ¾" x ¾"

Casters (4)

Did You Know...

The History of the Little Red Wagon

A traditional favorite, the little red wagon was made popular by Radio Flyer Inc., an American institution since 1917. By the 1930s the company was producing close to 1,500 wagons a day, working by the motto "For every boy. For every girl." In celebration of its 80th anniversary, Radio Flyer built the world's largest wagon (right): 27 feet long, 21 feet high, and more than 7 tons in weight!

Crosscut saw

Saber saw

Tongue-and-groove pliers

Long-nose pliers

Ratchet and socket set

Clamps

Rasp

Marking the angled sides

Once all the pieces of the wagon have been cut to size, the sides have to be marked and cut to the required angles.

♦ Measuring from one end of a side piece, make a mark 3 inches along one edge.

♦ With a straightedge, draw a line across the face of the board between the mark and the opposite corner *(left)*.

♦ Mark an identical line at the other end of the board, this time measuring along the opposite edge. Then, mark angled lines on the other side piece the same way.

Woodworking Tip

Before getting too far ahead in the project, it's a good idea to label the inside and outside faces of each piece. This will help avoid confusion and mistakes later on.

Cutting the angles

♦ Clamp one of the side pieces to your worktable with the marked line overhanging the table and parallel to the table's edge.

♦ Cut along the line with a crosscut saw *(right)*. Repeat for the other side piece.

Rounding the corners

Rounding the corners of the sides will eliminate sharp edges and give the wagon a more finished appearance.

- Lay a can or lid about 2 inches in diameter against what will be the top front corner of one side piece. Trace the arc onto the board.

- Clamp the side piece to the table with the marked corner overhanging the edge by a few inches.

- With a rasp, file the corner down to the arc, working in even, downward strokes *(right)*. Round the diagonally opposite corner of the piece and the same two corners of the other side piece.

- Sand all four corners of both side pieces smooth with 120-grit sandpaper.

3/4"   3/4"

INSIDE FACE

Marking the position of the back and front pieces

To make it easier to assemble the wagon later on, mark where the back and front pieces will meet the sides.

- Lay one of the sides on the table inside face up. With a try square, mark a line that is perpendicular to the edges from one unrounded corner to the opposite edge *(left)*. Mark a parallel line 3/4 inch away and a second set of parallel lines at the other end of the board *(inset)*. Mark two identical sets of lines on the other side piece.

5 Marking countersink holes on the side pieces

♦ Turn the side piece over and, referring the inset illustration below, make marks for countersink holes.

♦ Make the same marks on the other side piece *(right)*.

♦ On the front and back pieces, draw a line 1 inch from the bottom edge parallel to the edge. Then, mark the midpoint of the line and add two more marks 2 inches from each end. You will drill holes at these marks in step 8.

3/8"

OUTSIDE FACE

1 "

6 Fastening the cleats to the sides

Narrow strips called cleats are added to the sides to support the bottom of the wagon.

♦ Measure and mark pilot holes 1 inch from the ends of each cleat.

♦ Position a cleat on a side piece, centered between the ends and flush with the bottom edge. Mark its position. Apply wood glue to the cleat and clamp it in position to the side piece. Repeat for the other side.

♦ Fit a 1/16-inch bit in a drill and mark a depth of 1 inch on the bit with masking tape. Drill pilot holes into the cleats at the marks.

♦ Drive a 1 1/4-inch screw into each pilot hole *(right)*.

7

Assembling the back, front, and sides

◆ Apply a bead of glue along the ends of the back and front pieces *(left)*.

◆ With a helper, position the front and back pieces against the sides within the parallel lines you drew in step 4. Clamp the four pieces together firmly, tightening two clamps across the sides.

Drilling the countersink holes

◆ Fit a drill with a combination bit, adjust the depth to 1 inch, and drill a countersink hole at each mark on the sides that is aligned with the front or back *(right)*. Do not drill the holes along the bottom edges of the sides—these are intended for the bottom piece, which is not in place yet.

◆ Drive a 1 1/2-inch screw into each hole, securing the sides to the back and front.

8

9

Adding the bottom

♦ Undo the clamps from the sides.

♦ Fit the bottom piece into place *(right)*, making sure that it sits firmly against the cleats.

10

Fastening the bottom

♦ Clamp one side to the worktable.

♦ With the combination bit in the drill, countersink a hole at each marked point along the bottom edge of the side.

♦ Fasten the bottom to the side piece, driving a 1½-inch screw into each hole *(left)*.

♦ Reposition the clamps and the wagon on the table to fasten the bottom to the other pieces.

Marking the wheel locations

The front wheels are swiveling casters; the back ones are stationary.

♦ Undo the clamps and set the wagon upside down on the table.

♦ Position the wheel assemblies on the bottom, the swivel wheels at the front, the stationary ones at the back.

♦ Holding one assembly snugly in its corner, mark the bolt holes on the bottom piece *(left)*. Mark the other three wheel assemblies.

Up Close...

Fastening the wheels

♦ Clamp the wagon to the worktable, then fit the drill with a 3/8-inch bit. Drill through the bottom piece at each bolt mark.

♦ Unclamp the wagon and reposition one of the wheel assemblies, lining up the drilled holes in the bottom with the holes in the assembly.

♦ Holding the wheel in place, lift the wagon and feed a carriage bolt through one of the holes in the upper face of the bottom piece. Fasten the bolt by hand with its washer and hex nut.

♦ Install the remaining bolts on all four wheels, then tighten the bolts and nuts with a ratchet and socket *(right)*.

You can use an adjustable wrench to tighten the nuts that secure the wheels in place, but the recessed bottom will make it a little awkward. A ratchet with a socket will do the job much more easily.

13 Cutting the side rails

The side rails are parallel to the sides and have angled ends and rounded corners at the front.

♦ Measuring from one end of a side rail, make a mark 2 inches down along one edge. With a straightedge, draw a line across the face of the board between the mark and the opposite corner *(left)*.

♦ Clamp the rail to the table and cut along the line with a crosscut saw.

♦ Mark and cut the other side rail, then round the bottom front corner of each rail as you did for the side pieces in step 3.

Fastening the uprights to the wagon

14

♦ Measure and mark a centerline along the face of each of the four uprights.

♦ Mark two points on each line: 1/2 inch and 3 1/2 inches from the bottom ends.

♦ Clamp one of the uprights snugly in one back corner of the wagon with the marked points facing out.

♦ Drill countersink holes for 1 1/2-inch screws at both marks using the drill and combination bit. Drive screws into the holes.

♦ Clamp another upright 4 inches along the side from the first. Drill countersink holes and fasten it to the side piece *(right)*.

♦ Fasten the two remaining uprights to the other side piece.

Fastening the back rail

15

♦ Mark two countersink holes at each end of the back rail's outside face: 3/8 inch from the end, 1 inch from the edges.

♦ Apply a bead of wood glue on the back edges of the corner uprights. Clamp the back rail to the corner uprights so its top edge is flush with the uprights' top ends. Align the ends of the rail with the outside of the uprights.

♦ Drill a countersink hole with the combination bit at each mark, then drive 1 1/2-inch screws into the holes *(below)*.

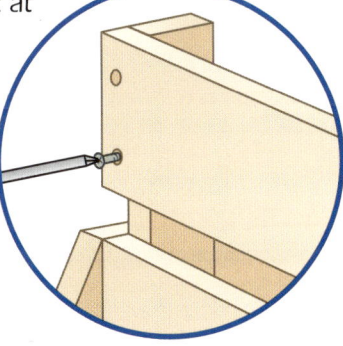

Although screws are the best fasteners for holding the back rail and uprights together, make sure the countersink holes are drilled straight; otherwise, the screws may pierce the sides of the uprights.

Attaching the side rails

16

♦ Mark four countersink holes on each side rail's outside face: one pair 1 3/4 inches from the back end, another 6 inches from the back end. Offset all the holes 1 inch from the edges.

♦ Apply a bead of glue on the outside face of the uprights, then clamp the side rails to them, aligning the top edge of the rails with the top end of the uprights. The back end of the side rails should be flush with the outside of the back rail.

♦ Drill a countersink hole with the combination bit at each mark, then drive 1 1/2-inch screws into the holes *(right)*.

Adding the handle support

Adding a handle support to the front of the wagon ensures that pulling the handle won't weaken the wagon's structure.

◆ Round the corners of the handle support using a sanding block fitted with 120-grit sandpaper.

◆ Find the center of the support by drawing diagonal lines between opposite corners. This is where the screw eye for the handle will be located.

◆ Mark a countersink hole on the support 1 inch from each corner.

◆ Center the support on the front, aligning the bottom edge of the pieces. Outline the support on the front.

◆ Apply wood glue to the back of the support, then clamp it in position to the front.

◆ Drill a countersink hole with the combination bit at each marked point *(right)*, then drive 1 1/2-inch screws into the holes.

17

18

Preparing the handle

◆ Fit a 3/16-inch bit in the drill and mark a depth of 1 inch on the bit with masking tape. Drill a pilot hole into the center of the handle support.

◆ Clamp the handle to the worktable and drill an identical pilot hole into the center of the end of the handle.

◆ Fasten one screw eye to the handle support on the wagon.

◆ With long-nose pliers, open the end of the other screw eye enough to join the two eyes together. Attach the second eye to the end of the handle. With screwdrivers, tighten both screw eyes until the threads disappear *(left)*.

Fastening the hand grip

19

♦ Round the edges of the hand grip with the sanding block.

♦ Find the center of the piece by drawing diagonal lines from opposite corners.

♦ Clamp the grip to a piece of scrap wood on the table, then drill a 1/16-inch hole through the center of the grip.

♦ With the handle clamped to the table, center the hand grip on the end of the shaft. Drive a 1 1/2-inch screw through the hole in the grip into the shaft *(right)*.

20

Attaching the handle to the wagon

♦ Hook the open screw eye on the handle onto the closed eye on the handle.

♦ With tongue-and-groove pliers, close the screw eye on the handle, locking the eyes together *(left)*.

♦ Get out some red paint and away you go!

Paint Your Wagon

A couple of coats of red paint will not only make your wagon look great and authentic. It will also help it last a lot longer! Make sure you choose an exterior paint. It will stand up well to moisture and extremes of temperature. Start with a coat of primer, then apply two coats of your final color. You'll get better results if you sand very lightly between coats with 180-grit paper. And don't forget to wipe off any dust with a damp rag. For a really professional job, cover the screw eyes, the wheel bases, and the heads of the carriage bolts with masking tape so you don't get paint on them.

Building a Toy Trolley

Are toys scattered all over the house? Picking them up—and moving them—is fun and easy with a toy trolley.

With heavy-duty casters and ample storage space, this toy box on wheels provides a perfect rolling home for dozens of toys. The sides, ends, and bottom are made from MDF (medium-density fiberboard). It's strong and smooth, but the pieces are too big to cut by hand. Get someone at the store to cut them to size for you from a 4x8-foot sheet. Once the trolley is assembled, you can stencil on a name or design, or just let your imagination direct the paintbrush. That's part of the fun!

Materials you'll need

Wood	1 4x8-foot sheet ⅝-inch MDF (cut to dimensions shown in diagram opposite) 3 feet 1x3 pine 9 feet 1x1 pine
Hardware	4 2-inch heavy-duty swivel casters
Fasteners	#6 1-inch round-head screws #8 ¾-inch screws
Miscellaneous	Wood glue

The tools you'll need...

Screwdrivers
Hammer

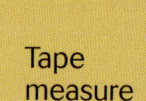
Try square

Tape measure

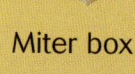
Miter box

Backsaw

How the pieces fit together...

- The ends and bottom are screwed to cleats mounted to the sides of the box.

- The wheel supports are screwed to the sides and bottom. Swivel casters are mounted to the underside of the supports.

End panels (2)
18" x 17" x 5/8"

Bottom panel
26 1/4" x 18" x 3/4"

End cleats (4)
15 1/2" x 3/4" x 3/4"

Side panels (2)
30" x 18" x 5/8"

Casters (4)

Wheel supports (2)
18" x 2 1/2" x 3/4"

Bottom cleats (2)
21" x 3/4" x 3/4"

Did You Know...

What is MDF?

MDF is short for medium-density fiberboard. It's a composite sheet product commonly used as a substitute for solid wood. Made of specially "cooked" wood fibers, MDF is hot-pressed into a mat and sanded smooth. This makes it extremely strong and stable, and it tends to resist warping and cracking. It also takes paint well and doesn't splinter. MDF usually comes in sheets 4 feet wide by 8 feet long and in different thicknesses, from 1/8 inch to 1 inch. It is widely used in making furniture, cabinets, toys, shelving, doors, and flooring.

Crosscut saw

Saber saw

Electric drill with 1/16-inch twist bit

Straightedge

Clamps

Marking the curved corners on the sides

The corners of the side panels are rounded to eliminate sharp edges. The simplest way to mark the curves is with a can. For the curve shown, use a can with roughly a 2¼-inch radius—a large soup can will usually do the trick.

♦ Hold the can at one corner of a side panel so its rim touches both edges of the panel. Trace the rim of the can to mark the curve *(left)*. Repeat on the remaining corners of both side panels.

Cutting the curves

Cut the curved corners with a saber saw. Work slowly to avoid having the blade bind in the kerf and possibly break. Put the tool's power cord over your shoulder when you work to keep it out of the saw's cutting path.

♦ Clamp a side panel to your worktable with one corner overhanging the table's edge.

♦ Cut slowly along the marked line. Guide the tool carefully to keep the blade on line. Reposition the side panel to cut on the other corners of both panels *(right)*.

Cutting the cleats

♦ You can cut all the cleats to length from 1x1 stock. First, measure and mark the length of the cleats on the wood. Hold the piece in a miter box, lining up your cutting marks with the 90-degree slot. Make each cut with a backsaw *(left)*.

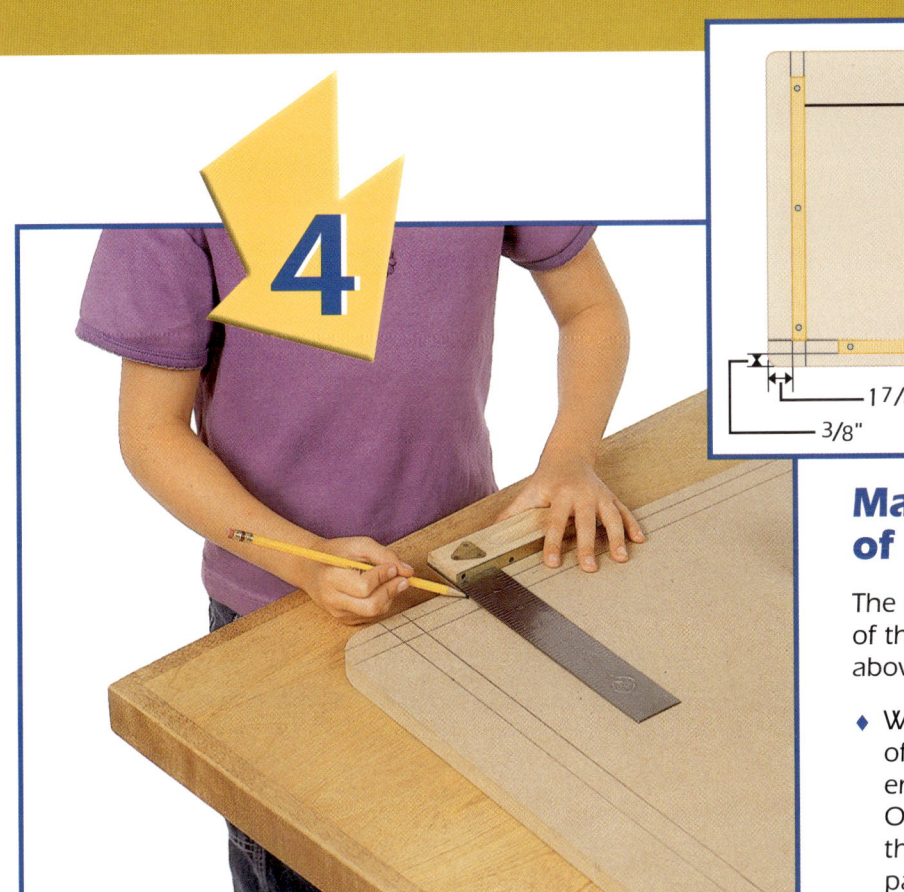

30"

End cleats

SIDE PANEL

18"

Bottom cleat

1 7/8" 4 1/2" 1 1/8"

3/8"

Marking the locations of the cleats

The cleats are installed on the inside face of the side panels. Refer to the diagram above to mark the cleat locations.

♦ Write "top" and "bottom" on the inside of both side panels so you know which end is up when you assemble the trolley. Outline each cleat by measuring from the edge of the panel and making a pair of marks for the inside and outside edges of the cleat. Connect the marks with a straightedge. Then, measure and mark the end of each cleat with a try square *(left, above)*.

Preparing the cleats for gluing

For extra strength, the cleats are fastened with glue and screws.

♦ Apply a thin bead of wood glue along an edge of one of the bottom cleats *(right)*. Spread the glue with a wooden popsicle stick or stir stick.

6

Drilling pilot holes in the cleats

♦ Clamp the bottom cleat to a side panel, aligned within the outline drawn in step 4.

♦ Mark four evenly spaced points along the length of the cleat for the screws.

♦ Install a 1/16-inch bit in an electric drill and mark a depth of 5/8 inch on the bit with masking tape. Drill a pilot hole into the cleat at each mark, keeping the drill upright and stopping when the tape touches the cleat *(left)*.

Fastening the cleats to the side panels

7

♦ Drive 1-inch round-head screws through each hole in the cleat and into the side panel *(right)*. Repeat steps 5 to 7 to install the remaining cleats on both side panels.

8

Drilling pilot holes in the end panels

♦ Mark two guidelines along the outside face of each end panel, each one 3/8 inch from the edges.

♦ Clamp a side panel outside-face down to the table. Position one of the end panels against an end cleat so its bottom end is flush with the bottom edge of the side panel. Clamp the end panel to the cleat, using small wood pads to prevent damaging the panel. Then, mark four evenly spaced points along the line opposite the side-panel cleat. Offset the points from the screws holding the cleat to the side panel.

♦ Drill a pilot hole into the end panel at each mark *(left)*.

Attaching the end panel

♦ Drive 1-inch round-head screws into the holes you drilled in step 8 to secure the end panel to the side *(above)*. Install the second end panel to the other end cleat the same way.

9

Something Screwy

For hundreds of years, all screws had a plain slotted head. In fact, the standard slotted screw is thought to date back to the early 16th century. But after the blade of a new screwdriver he was demonstrating slipped from the slot of a screw and hurt his hand, a Canadian traveling salesman and part-time inventor named Peter Robertson got an idea. In 1907 he patented a new screw with a square head that the blade of a screwdriver would fit into without slipping. Called the Robertson screw, it is used today mostly in Canada and by a number of American woodworkers and other craftsmen. In the U.S., the Phillips screw, patented by Oregon businessman Henry F. Phillips in the early 1930s, is the screw of choice. With its star-shaped head, the screw also resists slipping. By the end of the decade, the Phillips was the favored screw of big industry. Today a minor controversy rages over which screw is best. Try them all and judge for yourself.

 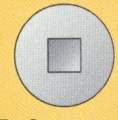 

Slotted   **Robertson**   **Phillips**

Fastening the second side

♦ With the two end panels fastened to one side panel, simply set the second side panel on the end pieces, aligning its bottom edge with those of the end panels. Mark and drill pilot holes through the end panels into the cleats and drive screws to secure the assembly *(right)*.

10

Trimming the corners of the bottom panel

11

The corners of the bottom panel are removed to accommodate the 3/4-inch by 3/4-inch end cleats.

♦ Outline a 3/4-inch square at each corner of the bottom panel. Then, cut along the marks with a crosscut saw to remove the corners *(right)*. Cut all four corners of the bottom panel.

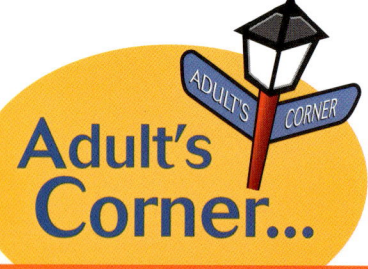

Adult's Corner...

Installing the bottom panel

12

Drilling pilot holes for the screws that secure the bottom panel can be tricky, especially for young woodworkers. The cleats on the side panels are narrow, so you'll have to hold the drill up close to the sides while you work. This can be a little awkward, so drill the holes yourself, holding the drill as straight as possible. Make sure to point out the importance of a steady hand and good positioning to your young apprentice. He or she can drive the screws in by hand once the pilot holes are made.

♦ Position the bottom panel on its cleats, then mark four evenly spaced points along each edge and three along each end. Offset the points by 3/8 inch from the side and end panels. Also offset them from the screws holding the bottom cleats in place.

♦ Drill a pilot hole into the bottom panel at each mark *(right)*. Then, drive 1-inch round-head screws into the holes to secure the bottom.

Attaching the wheel supports

13

The casters are mounted on wheel supports screwed to the end and bottom panels.

♦ Turn the box on one side and mark two evenly spaced points on the end panels 3/8 inch from the bottom. Set a wheel support flat on the bottom panel, flush against one end panel. Using the drill fitted with a 1/16-inch bit, drill a pilot hole into the end panel at each point that is aligned with the wheel support.

♦ Holding the wheel support in place, drive a screw into each hole in the end panel *(right)*. Install the other support against the opposite end panel.

14

Installing the casters

The casters are screwed to the underside of the wheel supports 3/4 inch from the corners of the trolley.

♦ Make a pair of position marks at each corner, 3/4 inch from the end and side panels.

♦ Align each caster's mounting plate with its marks and mark the holes in the plate on the wheel support *(left)*.

♦ Drill a pilot hole into the wheel support at each point, marking a depth of 1/2 inch on the bit with masking tape. Screw the casters in place with 3/4-inch screws.

Securing the wheel to the bottom panel

15

The support blocks are also fastened to the bottom panel.

♦ Set the trolley on its casters and mark four evenly spaced points at each end of the bottom 1 inch from the end.

♦ Drill a pilot hole into the bottom at each mark, then drive screws through the bottom into the wheel supports *(right)*.

Building an Easel

The two painting boards on this easel adjust up or down, so you can share the fun with a younger brother or sister.

The easel isn't hard to make. The project is mostly sawing wood, drilling holes, tightening screws, and hammering nails. But you'll need help from an adult to get the wood pieces cut to the right size. Painting the easel will protect it so you can leave it outdoors.

Materials you'll need

Wood	26 inches x 19 inches ¼-inch plywood
	22 inches x 4 inches ¼-inch plywood
	36 feet 1x3 pine
	1 foot 2x4 pine
Hardware	12 2-inch thumbturn bolts and wing nuts
	2 15-inch lengths lightweight chain
	2 2-inch butt hinges
Fasteners	#6 1¼-inch screws
	#6 ¾-inch screws
	¾-inch common nails
Miscellaneous	Wood glue

The tools you'll need...

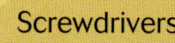
Screwdrivers

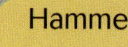
Hammer

Clamps

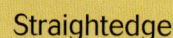
Straightedge

Tape measure

How the pieces fit together...

- The painting boards hang on thumbturn bolts that fit through the legs and battens.

- The legs have a row of holes so you can hang each board at the best height for whoever is using the easel.

- The legs are attached at the top with hinges, which lets them open or close flat.

- Chains between the legs hold the easel open.

- The feet are cut at an angle so they sit flat on the ground.

- The trays are screwed and nailed together.

- The V-shaped wedges go between the trays and the legs so the trays don't tilt.

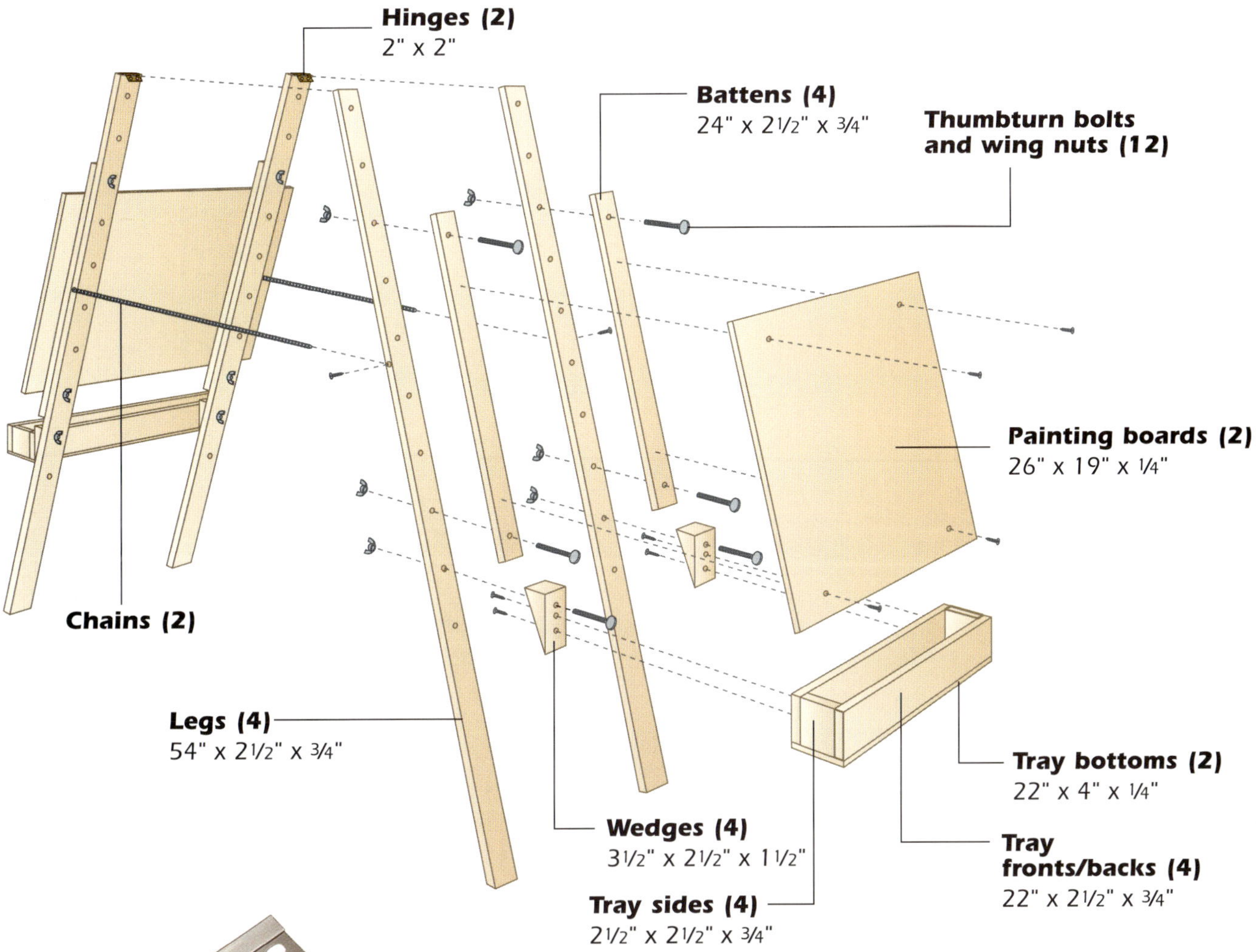

Hinges (2)
2" x 2"

Battens (4)
24" x 2½" x ¾"

Thumbturn bolts and wing nuts (12)

Painting boards (2)
26" x 19" x ¼"

Chains (2)

Legs (4)
54" x 2½" x ¾"

Wedges (4)
3½" x 2½" x 1½"

Tray sides (4)
2½" x 2½" x ¾"

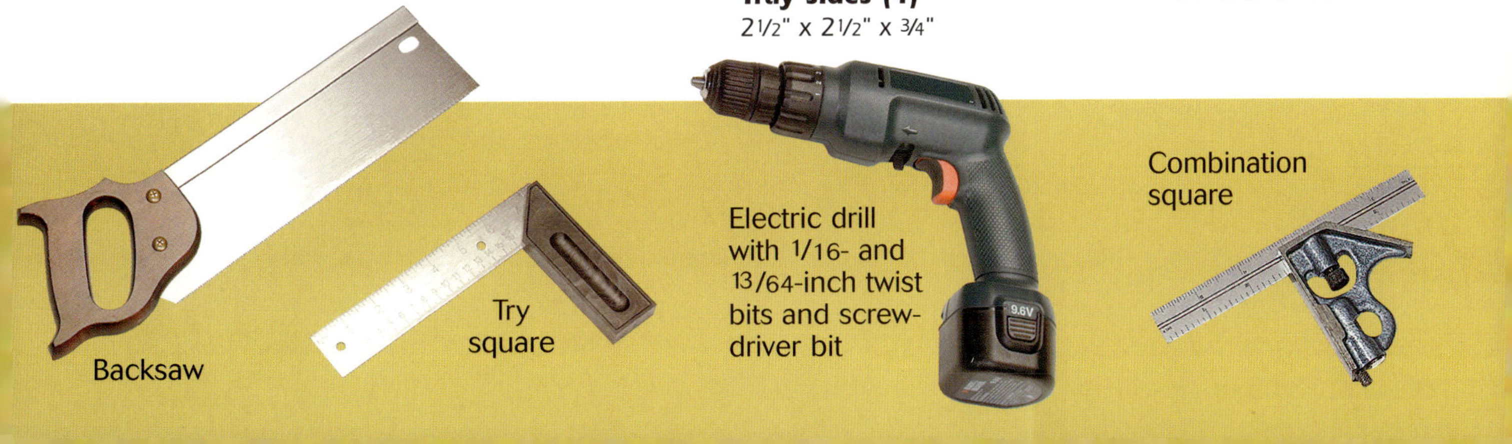

Tray bottoms (2)
22" x 4" x ¼"

Tray fronts/backs (4)
22" x 2½" x ¾"

Backsaw

Try square

Electric drill with 1/16- and 13/64-inch twist bits and screw-driver bit

Combination square

Marking the angled cuts on the feet

- ◆ Cut all the pieces of the easel to size.

- ◆ On the edge of one leg, measure ¼ inch from the end and make a mark at that point.

- ◆ Draw a diagonal line across the edge from the mark to the opposite corner.

- ◆ Use a combination square or try square to extend the line straight across the face of the board *(left)*.

- ◆ Mark the three other legs this way.

Cutting the angled feet

- ◆ Clamp a leg to a piece of scrap wood on your worktable so the diagonal line you marked on the edge is facing up.

- ◆ Cut through the leg along the line with a backsaw *(right)*. Keep the blade perfectly straight and even with your line.

- ◆ Cut the other feet the same way.

Marking the bolt holes on the legs

- ◆ Measure and mark the center of one leg's wide face in two places. Then, use a straightedge to draw a line from the one end of the leg to the other, passing through both marks.

- ◆ Starting at the top, measure 2 inches along the line and make a mark; then, make another mark every 4 inches *(left)* until you have made 10 marks.

- ◆ Mark one of the other legs the same way.

Drilling the holes

♦ Place one of the unmarked legs on a piece of scrap wood on your worktable, then clamp a marked leg on top so the two legs line up.

♦ Fit your electric drill with a 13/64-inch bit and drill bolt holes through both legs at the marks *(right)*.

♦ Drill the other two legs the same way.

4

5

Fastening the painting boards to the battens

♦ Lay two battens on the table and place a painting board on top so it overlaps the battens at the corners as shown at left.

♦ Install a 1/16-inch bit in the drill and mark a depth of 1/2 inch on it with masking tape. Drill a pilot hole through the painting board and into the batten near each corner.

♦ Fasten the painting board to the battens with 3/4-inch screws *(left)*.

♦ Attach the second board to the two other battens.

Drilling holes in the battens

♦ Turn over the painting board and battens and slip a piece of scrap wood under them.

♦ Place a leg over one of the battens so there are are three bolt holes both above and below the painting board. Clamp the pieces securely to the worktable.

♦ With the 13/64-inch drill bit, extend every bolt hole in the legs through the battens and into—but not through—the boards *(right)*.

Making the paint trays

♦ Clamp the back across the sides of one tray, making sure the ends and edges line up.

♦ Switch to the 1/16-inch bit and mark a depth of 5/8 inch on the bit with masking tape. Drill two pilot holes through the back into each side, then drive in 1 1/4-inch screws.

♦ Add the front and make the other tray *(left)*.

Adding the paint tray bottoms

♦ Lay the bottom piece of one of the trays in place, making sure it lines up with the sides, front, and back.

♦ Drive a 3/4-inch common nail into each corner, then evenly space three other nails along the front and back.

♦ Nail the bottom on the other tray *(right)*.

Up Close...

Sawing the wedges

- Mark a diagonal line across the edge of a 4-inch-long 2x4 between opposite corners.

- Use two small clamps to secure the 2x4 on a piece of scrap wood at one corner of the table so your cutting mark is facing up.

- Cut the block in half with a backsaw, keeping the blade in line with the cutting mark *(right)*.

- Saw a second pair of wedges.

9

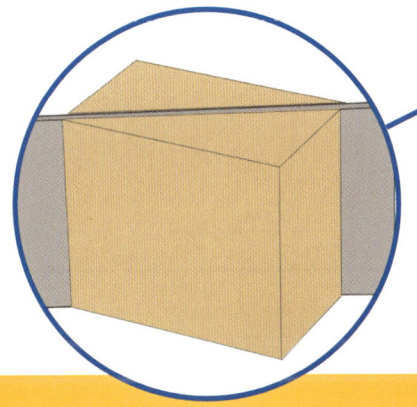

Cutting from one corner to the opposite corner of a 2x4 standing on edge will give you two equal wedges. Keep the saw perfectly vertical to make sure you stay on line for the whole cut.

10

Clamping the wedges for drilling

- Take one of the legs and make a mark 3/4 inch above any one of the bolt holes.

- Line up the thick end of a wedge with the mark *(left)* and clamp the pieces together.

Drilling the holes

- Turn over the leg and wedge and clamp them down.

- Slip a 13/16-inch bit into the hole in the leg and drill through the wedge *(left)*.

- Repeat for the other wedges. (You'll use these holes to attach the trays in step 16.)

11

Attaching the wedges to the trays

- Place a tray on its front and lay a wedge on the back, even with one side. Align the wedge's thin end with the tray's bottom.

- With the 1/16 bit, drill a pilot hole into a wedge near the thick end, wrapping masking tape around the bit 5/8 inch from the tip to keep you from drilling right through the tray. Drill another pilot hole near the thin end of the wedge.

- Screw the wedge in place with 3/4-inch screws at the thin end and 1 1/4-inch screws at the thick end *(right)*.

- Repeat this step to install the other wedges.

12

Marking holes for the leg hinges

♦ Center one leaf of a hinge on the straight end of a leg and mark its screw holes *(right)*.

♦ Repeat for the other three legs.

♦ Drill a 1/16-inch pilot hole into the end of the leg at each mark.

Attaching the hinges to the legs

♦ Stack two legs back to back. (Check that the angled ends form a V.)

♦ Fasten the hinges to the legs with 3/4-inch screws *(left)*.

♦ Hinge the other two legs together.

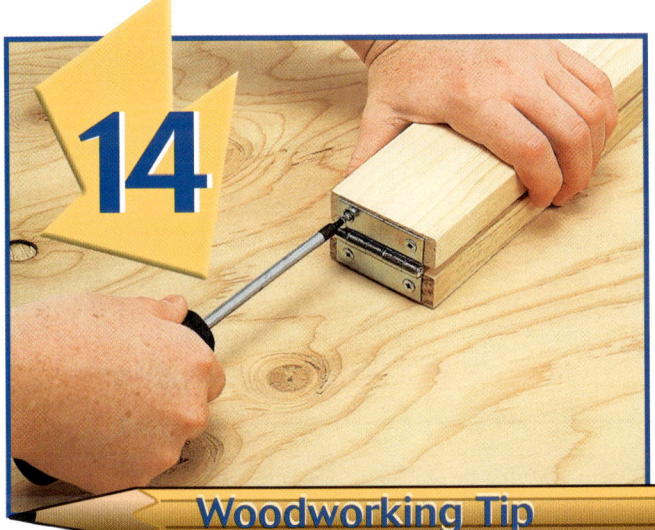

Woodworking Tip

You can buy screwdrivers with magnetic blades. They make it a lot easier to drive in a screw, especially if you need to have one of your hands free to hold the workpiece.

Fastening the painting boards to the legs

♦ Lay the legs side by side on the floor.

♦ Place a 2x4 on edge between each pair of legs to hold them open.

♦ Position a painting board on the legs so the holes in the battens and legs line up.

♦ Slip a thumbturn bolt through the top and bottom hole in each batten.

♦ Fit the wing nuts on the bolts and tighten them.

♦ Turn over the easel and fasten the other painting board *(right)*.

16 Hanging the paint trays

- Slip a thumbturn bolt through each hole in the wedges of a paint tray.

- Slide the bolts through the leg holes just below the battens *(left)*.

- Add the wing nuts, then attach the second tray.

Adding the chain

- Mark a point on the outer edge of each leg 18 inches from the top.

- Attach the chains to the legs at each point by drilling a pilot hole and securing the chain in place with ¾-inch screws *(right)*.

Personalizing Your Easel

One way to make your easel extra-special is to make custom-designed trays. The one shown at left holds baby food jars—they make great containers for paint. Before making the trays *(step 7)*, measure and mark where the jars will sit against the front and back. Then, ask an adult to make curved cuts at the marks to match the shape of the jars. The cuts can be made with an electric drill and a hole saw attachment. Once the cuts are finished, test fit the pieces of the tray with the jars so they fit snugly in place. You may have to trim the trays' sides a little.

Chapter 2

Backyard Projects

Building a **Birdhouse**

This project is simply for the birds! The entrance hole is just the right size for your favorite winged visitor, and the roof opens up so you can spring-clean each year.

A good project for kids as young as 8 years old, this birdhouse has all the right stuff, including metal mesh on the inside to help young birds get in and out of the box, and good ventilation to keep them cool in summer.

Materials you'll need

Wood	3 feet 1x6 cedar (or pine if painted)
Hardware	2 1-inch x 1-inch galvanized hinges 2½ inches square hardware cloth Pole mount
Fasteners	1-inch galvanized finishing nails #8 ¾-inch galvanized screws ½-inch double-pointed tacks

The tools you'll need...

Screwdrivers

Hammer

Tape measure

Awl

Hand drill with 1/32-inch twist bit

Clamp

How the pieces fit together...

- The sides, back, front, and bottom are nailed together.

- The sides are 1/8 inch shorter than the front and back, creating an air space for ventilation.

- The roof is attached to the back with hinges, and extends 1 inch past the front to prevent rain from getting inside.

- The top end of the back and front panels are cut at an angle so the slanted roof sits flat against them.

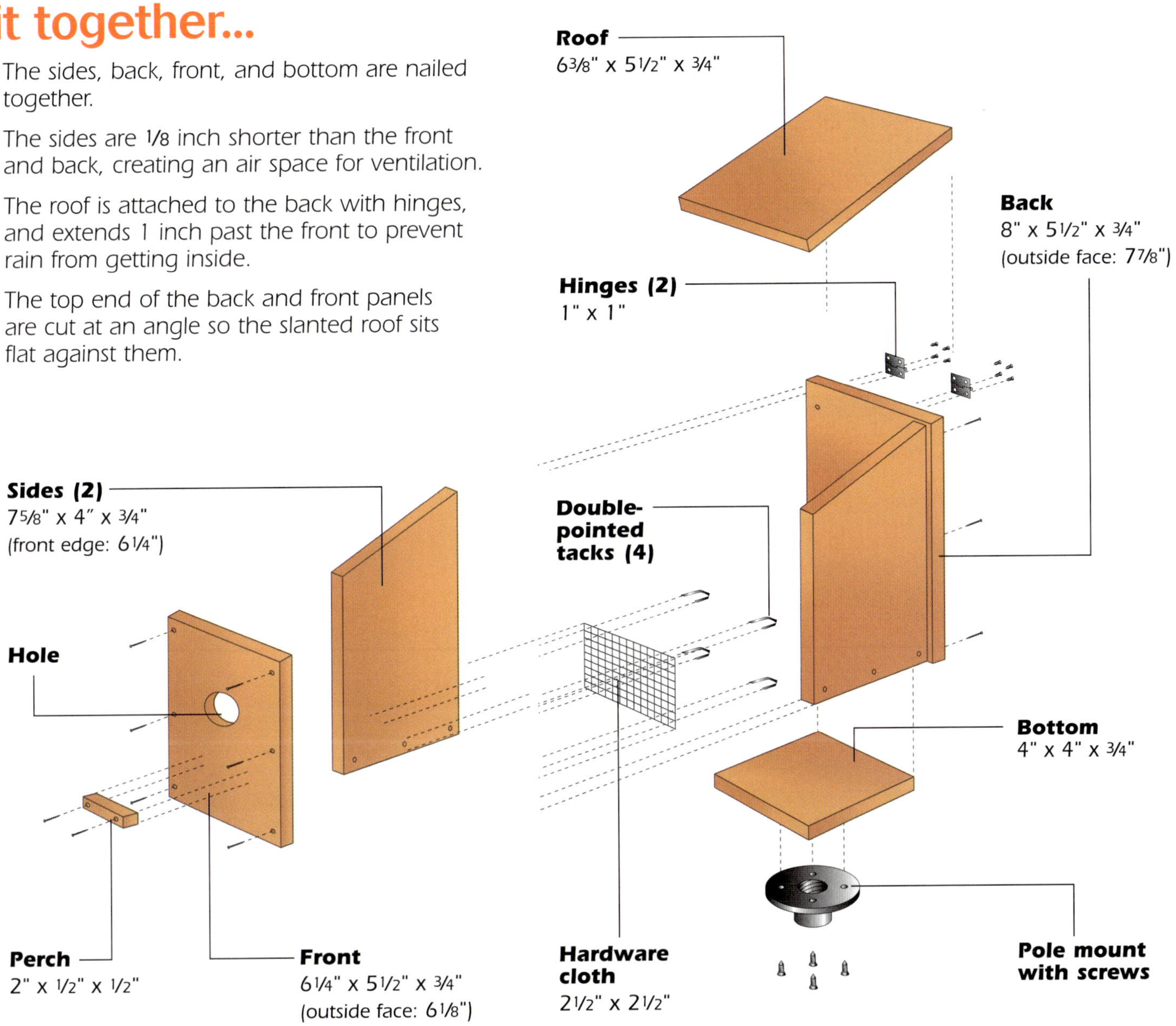

Roof
6³/8" x 5¹/2" x ³/4"

Back
8" x 5¹/2" x ³/4"
(outside face: 7⁷/8")

Hinges (2)
1" x 1"

Sides (2)
7⁵/8" x 4″ x ³/4"
(front edge: 6¹/4")

Double-pointed tacks (4)

Hole

Bottom
4" x 4" x ³/4"

Perch
2" x ¹/2" x ¹/2"

Front
6¹/4" x 5¹/2" x ³/4"
(outside face: 6¹/8")

Hardware cloth
2¹/2" x 2¹/2"

Pole mount with screws

Saber saw

Tin snips

Backsaw

Try square

Nail set

Electric drill with ¹/16-inch twist bit and hole saw

Cutting the sides

The top edge of the sides has to be cut at an angle so that the roof will slope properly.

♦ Mark a point on one edge of a side piece 6¼ inches from the bottom and another point on the other edge 7⅝ inches from the bottom. Join the marks with a line.

♦ Clamp one of the sides to a piece of scrap wood on your worktable.

♦ Line up the blade of a backsaw with the marked line and cut through the side.

♦ Cut the other side the same way *(left)*.

Drilling the opening in the front

Different kinds of birds need a different-sized opening for their house, as you can see in the chart below.

♦ Measure and mark the midpoint of the bottom and top ends of the front piece. Join the marks with a vertical line. Then, make a short horizontal line 2½ inches down from the top end. The center of your hole will be where the two lines cross.

♦ Clamp the front to a piece of scrap wood on the table.

♦ Fit your power drill with a hole saw the same size as the opening you want. Line up the hole saw with the center mark and drill the hole *(right)*.

The hole story

A tiny house wren needs a smaller hole than a much bigger bird such as a purple martin. Here is the size of opening you'll need for some popular birds:

House wren	1 inch
Chickadee	1⅛ inches
Nuthatch	1⅜ inches
Bluebird	1⁹⁄₁₆ inches
Purple martin	2¼ inches

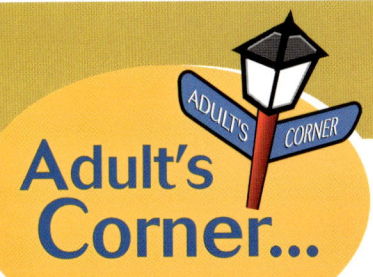

Adult's Corner...

Making angled cuts

3

Cut the top end of the front and back pieces of the birdhouse with a saber saw. Because the blade cuts through more wood when cutting at an angle, use a slower rate of feed than usual.

- To adjust the cutting angle of a saber saw, undo the nut that secures the base plate. Hold the angled top end of a side piece *(step 1)* against the plate and swivel the plate to the same angle. Then, tighten the base-plate nut.
- Measure and mark the outside face of the back of the birdhouse (8 inches) on a 1x6.
- Clamp the board to the table with the mark extending 2 inches past the edge of the table.
- Make the cut with the blade of the saw angled away from the table *(right)*.
- Cut the front the same way so its outside face measures 6¼ inches.

4

Assembling the bottom and sides

- Mark three evenly spaced points on one of the side pieces 3/8 inch from the bottom.
- Clamp the board to a piece of scrap wood on the table.
- Fit a drill with a 1/32-inch bit and drill a hole through the board at each mark *(left)*.
- Cut the bottom of the birdhouse to size, place it on edge on the table, and clamp one of the side pieces to it so the edges align. Make sure the bottom end of the side is flush with the bottom's outside face.
- With a hammer, drive a 1-inch finishing nail into each hole in the side. Sink the nail heads below the surface of the wood with the hammer and a nail set.
- Fasten the other side piece to the bottom the same way.

Attaching the hardware cloth

Hardware cloth isn't really cloth at all, but a kind of wire mesh. Attaching it to the inside of the front will help young birds get in and out.

♦ With tin snips, cut a piece of mesh 2½ inches square.

♦ Set the front outside-face down and center the mesh under the opening. Fasten the mesh in place by tapping in a double-pointed tack at each corner *(above)*.

Assembling the front and back

♦ Draw two guidelines along the length of the back piece ½ inch from each edge. Then, mark four evenly spaced points along each line.

♦ Clamp the board to a piece of scrap wood on the table and drill a hole through it at each mark.

♦ Center the back piece on the sides so its bottom end is flush with their edges.

♦ Fasten the back to the sides by driving a nail into each hole. Sink the nail heads.

♦ Attach the front to the sides *(above)*, driving only three nails per side.

Attaching the perch

♦ Mark a short line on the front ½ inch below the opening.

♦ Extend the line across the front, using a try square to make sure the line is perpendicular to the edges.

♦ Cut the perch to size, clamp it to a piece of scrap wood on the table, and drill a hole through it ½ inch from each end.

♦ Center the perch under the opening in the front, aligning its top edge with the marked line. Then, drive a nail into each hole in the perch to anchor it in place *(left)*. Sink the nail heads.

You can hold a nail steady with your fingers for the first couple of taps, but once it's standing on its own, move your fingers away.

8

Hinging the top to the back

- Lay the birdhouse face down on the table, propping the bottom end on a piece of scrap wood.

- Clamp the top to the sides so the edges of all three pieces are flush; make sure the back end of the top is flush with the back panel.

- Set one hinge 1/2 inch from the edges of the sides and top, its pin centered between them and the leaves flat on the panels. Outline the leaves on the panels, then mark their screw holes *(right)*. Mark the other hinge 1/2 inch from the opposite edges.

- Remove the hinges, then punch a starter hole into the wood at each mark with an awl.

- Hold the hinges within their marked outlines and fasten them in place with the screws supplied.

9

Adding the pole mount

- Lay the birdhouse upside down on the table.

- Center the pole mount on the bottom and mark its screw holes. Remove the mount. Fit a drill with a 1/16-inch bit and mark a depth of 1/2 inch on it with masking tape. Drill a pilot hole into the bottom at each mark.

- Fasten the pole mount to the bottom with 3/4-inch screws *(left)*.

Building a Bike Rack

Tired of having nowhere to park your bicycle? That won't be a problem once you've built this neat bike rack. It can handle the whole family's wheels and will look great at the end of your driveway.

With ample space for up to five bikes of any size, this rack has the strength and stability to stand on its own. But it's also light enough to move around. Once the rack is built, protect it from the elements with some good-quality exterior paint or stain, or a couple of coats of water sealer.

Materials you'll need

Wood	17 feet 2x4 pine
	19 feet 2x2 pine
Fasteners	#8 1¼-inch deck screws
	#8 1½-inch deck screws
	#8 2½-inch deck screws

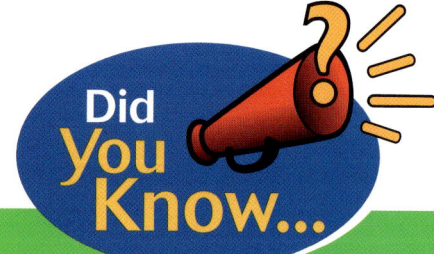

Did You Know...

The Wheel Story

Leonardo da Vinci was a busy man. When he wasn't painting masterpieces such as the Mona Lisa, he was dreaming up inventions such as the helicopter—and the bicycle. He sketched a design for a primitive bike in 1490. However, it wasn't until 1817 that a German baron actually built a working bicycle that could be steered. The baron used his

The tools you'll need...

Try square

Crosscut saw

Clamps

Tape measure

Ripsaw

How the pieces fit together...

♦ Six 2x4 uprights spaced 3½ inches apart are fastened between 2x2 top and bottom rails.

♦ A 2x4 brace joined to each end of the bottom rail by an interlocking half-lap helps to make the rack stable.

♦ Two 2x2 outer rails screwed to the ends of the braces add stability.

♦ Angled 2x2 end supports between the top and outer rails anchor the corners of the rack.

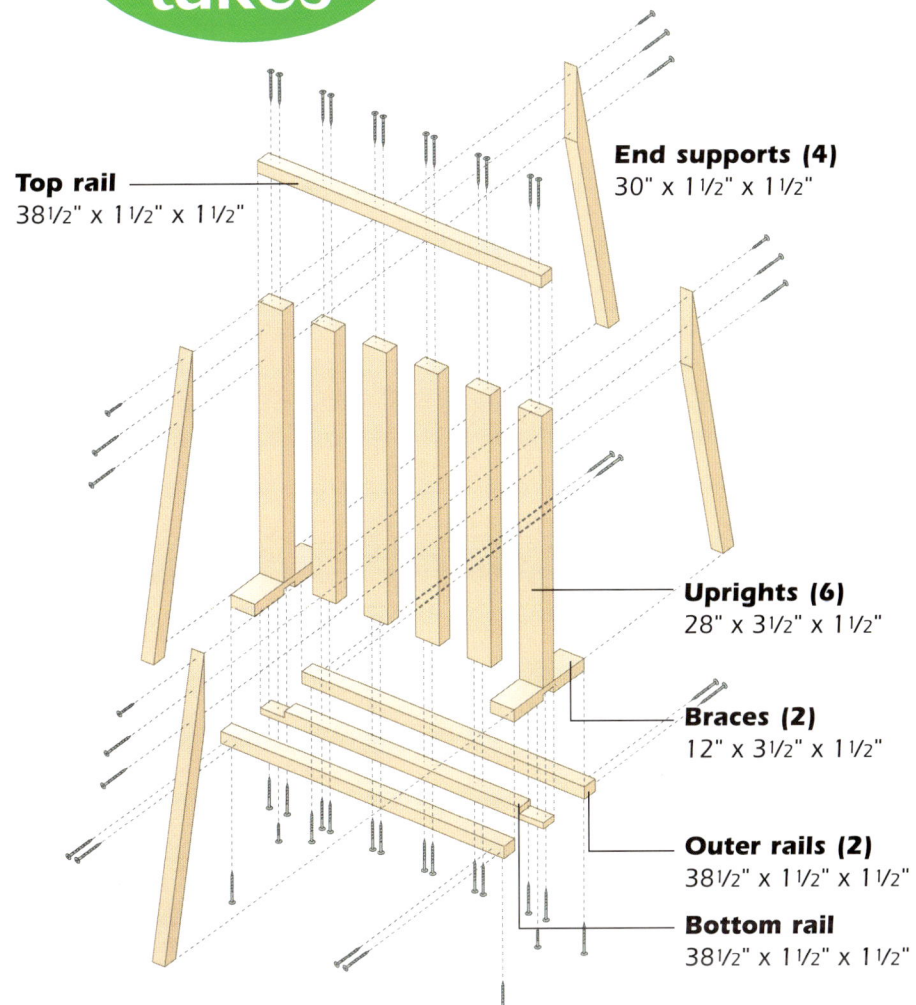

Top rail
38½" x 1½" x 1½"

End supports (4)
30" x 1½" x 1½"

Uprights (6)
28" x 3½" x 1½"

Braces (2)
12" x 3½" x 1½"

Outer rails (2)
38½" x 1½" x 1½"

Bottom rail
38½" x 1½" x 1½"

feet, scooter-style, to push himself around on the wooden machine that was dubbed the "hobby horse." The 1860s saw the introduction of a two-wheeled riding machine with pedals connected to the front wheel. Some called it the "velocipede" (fast foot). Others labeled it the "bone-shaker" because of how it felt when the metal wheels—no tires!—went over cobblestones. Then, came the high-wheel bicycle. This funny-looking machine had a huge wheel in the front and a small one in the back, giving it the name "penny farthing" after the biggest and smallest coins then used in England. In the 1890s British engineers began to design the bicycles that we are used to seeing now, with front and back wheels of a matching size and a chain drive.

Backsaw

Sanding block and 120-grit sandpaper

Electric drill with 1/16-inch twist bit and screwdriver bit

Wood chisel

Wooden mallet

Outlining the width of the half-laps on the braces

The trickiest part of this whole project is cutting the interlocking notches, called half-laps, in the bottom rail and the two braces. The half-laps make for a strong joint that will keep the rack from wobbling.

◆ Cut the uprights, rails, and braces to length. Cut each of the four end supports about 36 inches long. (You'll trim them later in step 13.)

◆ Center the half-lap outlines on the braces between the ends: Lay a brace flat on your worktable, then measure and mark a point on each edge 6 inches from the ends. These points represent the center of the brace.

◆ Make a mark 3/4 inch to each side of these mid-points. With a try square, draw a line between the marks to one side of the midpoints, then join the marks on the other side. Keep the handle of the square against the edge of the brace so the lines are parallel (left). The two lines will guide you in cutting the width of the half-laps.

◆ Mark the width of a half-lap on the other brace.

Marking the depth of the half-laps

You'll need to cut the half-laps halfway through the braces.

◆ Lay a brace on edge on the table and, with the try square, mark a line on the edge that divides the board in half (right).

◆ Use the square to extend the lines from step 1 along the edge of the brace to the dividing line. These lines on the edge represent the depth of the half-lap.

◆ Mark the depth of the half-laps on the other edge of the brace and on both edges of the second brace.

Sawing the half-laps

- Clamp a brace to the table with the half-lap outline facing up.

- With a backsaw, cut along each line you marked in step 1, stopping when the cut reaches the depth lines marked in step 2. Concentrate on holding the saw as straight as possible and have a helper tell you when you reach the depth line.

- Make four or five more cuts between the first two *(left)*. Again, keep the saw straight and be careful not to cut beyond the depth lines.

Chiseling out the half-laps

- Undo the clamps and set the brace on edge. Hold a wood chisel straight up so the tip is on the depth line from step 2 and strike the handle with a wooden mallet to score the line. Turn the brace over and score the line on the other edge.

- Clamp the brace face up again. Hold the chisel at an angle, beveled side down *(inset)*, and strike it to chip waste from between the cuts *(right)*.

- Once most of the waste is gone, set the mallet aside and use the chisel beveled side up to shave the sides and bottom of the half-lap smooth. Cut and chisel the half-lap in the second brace.

Marking the bottom rail half-laps

The matching half-laps in the bottom rail can be made with just a couple of saw cuts.

- Slide one end of the bottom rail into one of the half-laps you cut in the braces. Make sure the end of the rail is flush with the edge of the brace. Slide the other end of the rail in the half-lap of the other brace.

- Run a pencil along the outline of the half-lap to mark the cut on the bottom rail *(left)*. Mark the half-lap on the other end of the rail.

Adult's Corner...

Cutting the half-laps in the bottom rails

The rip cut required here can be tricky to make. A perfectly straight cut along the length of the rail is an absolute must. To make it properly, keep the saw blade perfectly straight and make sure you follow your guidelines.

◆ Clamp the rail edge-up to the worktable with one of the outlines extending off the table. Start the cut with a ripsaw at a 60-degree angle *(right)*, keeping the blade aligned with the lines on both the edge and end of the rail *(inset)*. Finish the cut with the saw at a 90-degree angle so the kerf is flush with the end of the outline.

◆ Reposition the rail so it is face up on the table. Saw straight down from the face of the rail until the blade meets the first cut and the waste piece falls away. Cut the same half-lap at the other end of the rail.

6

7

Marking the upright locations on the top and bottom rails

◆ Place the top and bottom rails back to back on the work-table with their ends aligned.

◆ Align the edge of a scrap 2x4 with one end of the rails and trace the other edge on them. Repeat at the other end of the rails. The lines represent guidelines for the uprights.

◆ Move the 2x4 along the rails and mark another line, this time aligning the 2x4 with the previous line. Continue marking location lines for the uprights *(left)* until you reach the other end of the rails.

Woodworking Tip

To protect the teeth of your saw blade, cut a piece of foam pipe insulation slightly longer than the length of the blade. Slit one side of the foam with a utility knife, then wrap it around the blade. An elastic band helps hold the cover in place.

Attaching the bottom rail to the braces

The deck screws used to assemble the rack can be driven directly into the wood. If the wood has dried out, you can avoid splitting it by drilling countersink holes first *(see step 2, page 16)*.

♦ Fit the bottom rail and one of the braces together, then clamp the brace to the table. With an electric drill, drive a 1 1/4-inch screw through the center of the half-lap *(above)*, stopping when the screw head is flush with the wood surface. Fasten the other end of the rail to the second brace.

Fastening the uprights to the top rail

♦ Lay the top rail on edge on the table and position an upright against it so the edge of the upright is flush with the end of the rail. Clamp the boards in position to the table, then drive two 2 1/2-inch screws through the rail into the upright. Align the screws 3/4 inch from the edges of the upright. To avoid splitting in dry wood, drill countersink holes first. Attach the upright at the opposite end of the top rail the same way.

♦ Line up another upright with the second pair of guidelines made in step 7 and fasten it to the rail *(above)*. Attach the remaining uprights to the rail.

Attaching the uprights to the bottom rail

♦ With a helper holding the uprights steady, set the top rail down on the floor.

♦ Position the bottom rail on the uprights, aligning one end of the rail with the outside edge of the outer upright. Fasten the rail and upright together with a pair of 2 1/2-inch screws. Attach the opposite end of the rail to the other outer upright the same way.

♦ Fastened the remaining uprights to the bottom rail so the uprights line up with their guidelines *(left)*.

Attaching the outer rails to the braces

♦ Clamp the rack on one side to the table.

♦ Position an outer rail on the braces so the ends of the rail are flush with the outside edges of the braces. Holding the faces of the rail and braces flush, fasten the pieces together with a pair of 2½-inch screws at each end *(above)*. Turn over the rack and attach the other outer rail to the opposite end of the braces.

Adult's Corner...

Marking angles in the end supports

♦ Keep the rack on one side and place it with a brace overhanging the table. With a helper, center an end support against one end of both the top and outer rails.

♦ Run a pencil along the top rail and upright to mark an angled cutting line at one end of the support. Switch places with your helper and run the pencil along the outer rail to to mark the support's other end *(above)*. Mark the three other end supports the same way.

Cutting the end supports

A long angled cut through a 1½-inch-thick piece of wood can be a little tough for a youngster to do properly. You have to keep the blade of the saw perfectly straight and stay on the marked guideline through the entire cut.

♦ Clamp an end support down with the long angled cutting line overhanging the table. Make the cut with a ripsaw, keeping the blade lined up with the marked line throughout the cut *(right)*.

♦ Reposition the end support with its opposite end overhanging the table and clamp it in place. Cut the piece along the marked line, then cut both ends of the remaining supports.

Attaching the end supports to the uprights

◆ Set the rack on one side on the table again. Position an end support on the top and outer rails, its outside edges flush with the outside ends of the rails.

◆ With a helper holding the end support in position, attach its top end to the top rail with a 1¼-inch screw about 1 inch from the top. Drive a 2½-inch screw through the support about 5¼ inches below the first and a 1½-inch screw between the two screws *(left)*.

Attaching the end supports to the outer rails

◆ Holding the bottom of the end support in position, attach it to the outer rail with a 2½-inch screw *(right)*. Be careful to avoid the screws that hold the outer rail to the brace. Attach the remaining end supports.

◆ Sand off any rough spots or sharp edges with 120-grit sandpaper and a sanding block, then paint or stain the rack.

Building a Swing

For hours of fun outdoors, hang your swing from a sturdy tree branch—or, hang it indoors from the joists in a high ceiling.

Your swing can be ready in just a few hours. There's only one board to cut, a few holes to drill, a little paint to brush on, and two ropes to secure. Young swingers can help by measuring, shaping, and finishing the swing.

Materials you'll need

Wood	20 inches 2x8 pine or 7 1/2 inches x 1 1/2 inches hardwood
Hardware	2 4 1/2-inch x 5/8-inch screw eyes
Fasteners	1-inch common nails
Miscellaneous	2 lengths 1/2-inch rope (to reach from the seat to its perch) 4 rope clamps kraft paper

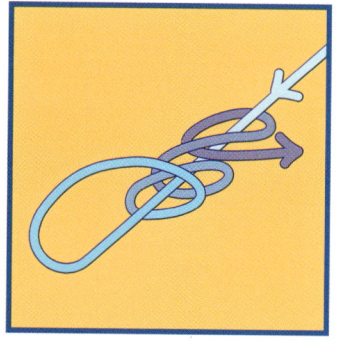

We use rope clamps to hang the swing. You can buy them at most big hardware stores. But you can also use a knot such as a rolling hitch *(left)*. It's a special knot used by sailors. Tied properly, it won't slip.

The tools you'll need...

Hammer

Tape measure

Clamps

Sanding block and 150-grit sandpaper

Crosscut saw

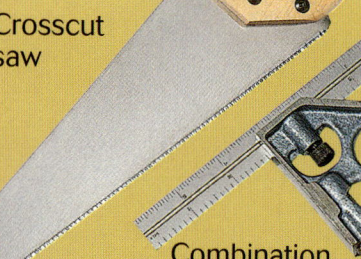
Combination square

The time it takes

½ hour to build
½ hour to paint

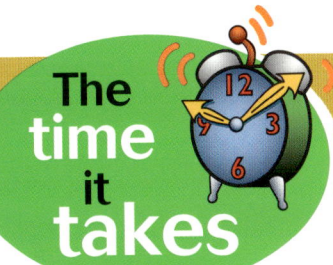

Marking the rope holes in the seat

- Cut the seat to size, then clamp it face up on your worktable.
- Adjust a combination square so the blade extends 3/4 inch from the handle.
- Holding the square flush against one end of the seat, mark a line on the piece.
- With the square against the edge, mark a second line that intersects the first.
- Repeat at the three other corners *(left)*.

2

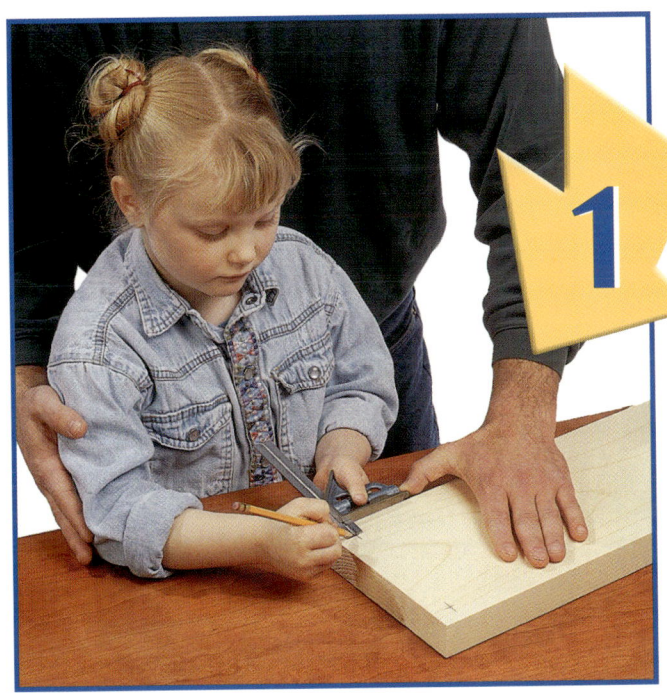

Drilling the holes

- Fit an electric drill with a 1/2-inch spade bit.
- Clamp the seat on a scrap board to protect your table.
- Drill a hole through the seat at each corner mark *(right)*.

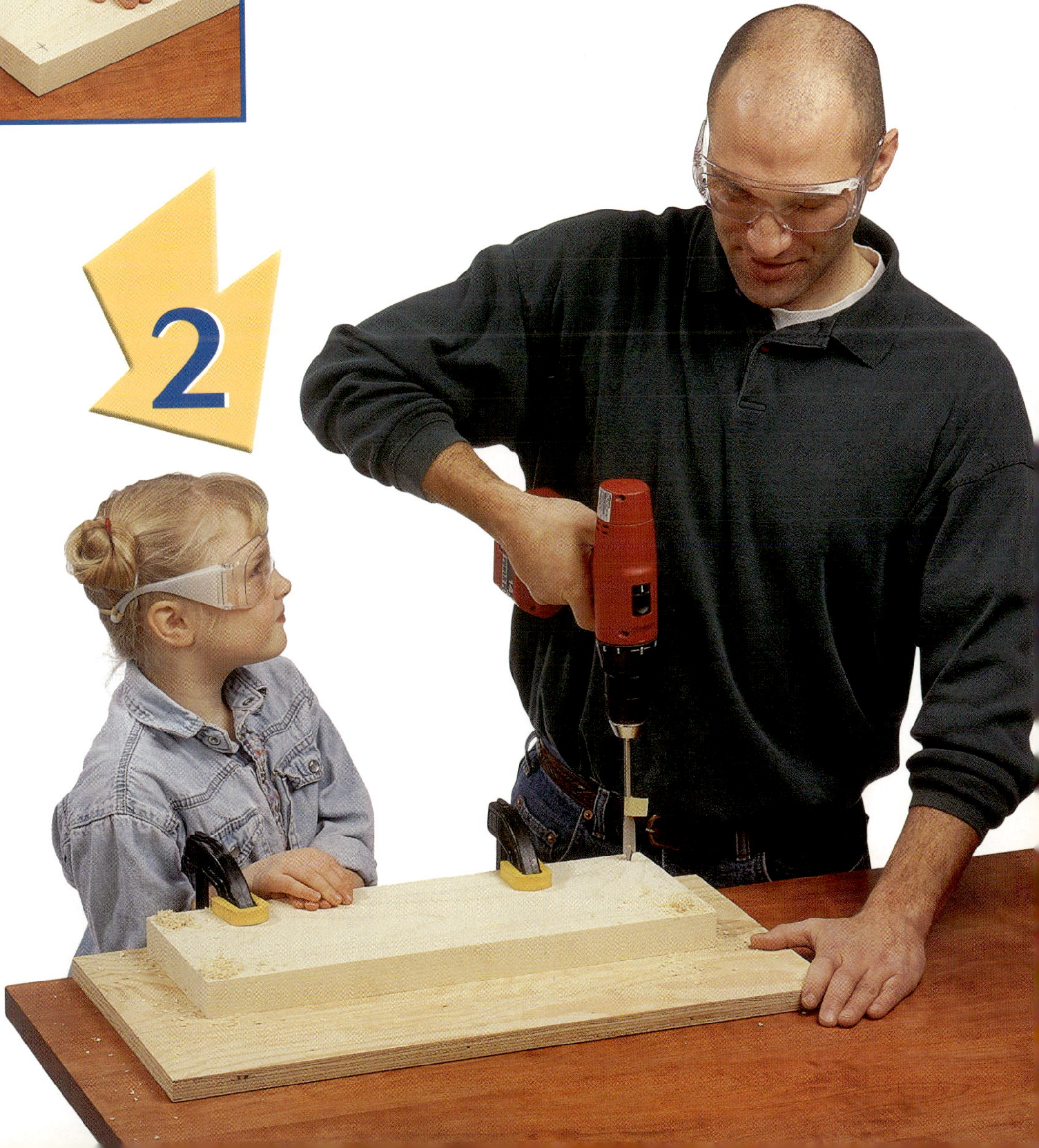

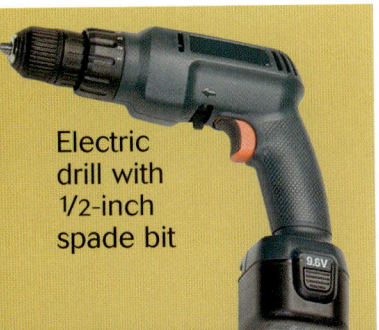

Electric drill with 1/2-inch spade bit

3

Shaping the seat

◆ Fit a sanding block with a piece of 150-grit sandpaper.

◆ Hold the sanding block at an angle to the seat, and work it back and forth, rounding over the top edges and corners *(right)*.

◆ Turn over the seat and smooth the other side.

4

Finishing the seat

◆ Place the seat on kraft paper on the bench.

◆ Cut four thin wood blocks and drive a 1-inch common nail through each one.

◆ Brush the finish on the top face of the seat, starting with a coat of primer *(left)*.

◆ Turn the seat over and set it on the nail tips—one at each corner.

◆ Finish the edges, ends, and other face of the seat.

◆ Let the finish dry, then reapply as many coats as suggested by the manufacturer.

5

Hanging the seat

- ♦ Unscrew the two pieces of a rope clamp and feed the first 18 inches of one rope through them.

- ♦ Feed the rope down through a hole in the seat and pass it up through the other hole on the same side.

- ♦ Push the free end of the rope through the pieces of the rope clamp so the rope is between the clamp teeth, then screw the clamp together *(above)*.

- ♦ Tie the second rope to the other side of the seat.

- ♦ Attach the top end of the ropes to a tree branch or to screw eyes screwed into a ceiling joist.

Choosing Rope

If you were hanging a swing 100 years ago, your choice of rope would have been pretty simple: basically, hemp, jute, or another natural material. But with the introduction of human-made fibers in the 20th century, the options since have grown a lot. Two good choices for the swing builder are polyester and nylon. Both types are strong and don't stretch. And both can be left outdoors without suffering ill effects. A 1/2-inch diameter rope will provide more than enough strength to support the biggest kid on the block.

Personalizing Your Swing

A simple coat or two of paint will make your swing look great and help it last longer. But if you want, there are lots of other options you can try. One choice is to stain your seat *(below, left)*. Another possibility is to make a stencil of some design such as a cat's face *(below, right)* and spray-paint it over your base coat. Whatever finish you apply, make sure it's designed for outdoor use.

Building a Picnic Table

Everyone enjoys a picnic, right? Well, you'll enjoy it even more if you have a table built especially for you and your friends, such as this half-scale beauty.

Build the table with cedar or pine and protect it with water sealer or a couple of coats of high-quality outdoor paint or stain. Then, sit it under a shady tree in your backyard. It's perfect for summer lunches, snacks, coloring, or playing games.

Materials you'll need

Wood	24 feet 2x6 pine or cedar
	33 feet 2x4 pine or cedar
Fasteners	3½-inch x ¼-inch carriage bolts
	#10 2½-inch deck screws
	#10 4-inch deck screws

The tools you'll need...

Tape measure

Hammer

Sanding block and 120-grit sandpaper

Crosscut saw

Screwdrivers

Carpenter's square

The time it takes

How the pieces fit together...

♦ Four 2x6s that form the tabletop are anchored to a cleat at each end of the table.

♦ The cleats are bolted to the four legs, which are angled at both ends to rest flush on the ground and the underside of the tabletop.

♦ A 2x4 seat support is fastened across the legs at each end of the table with carriage bolts.

♦ A 2x6 seat is attached to the seat supports on each side of the table.

♦ A pair of angled braces is fastened between the underside of the table and the seat supports to add stability.

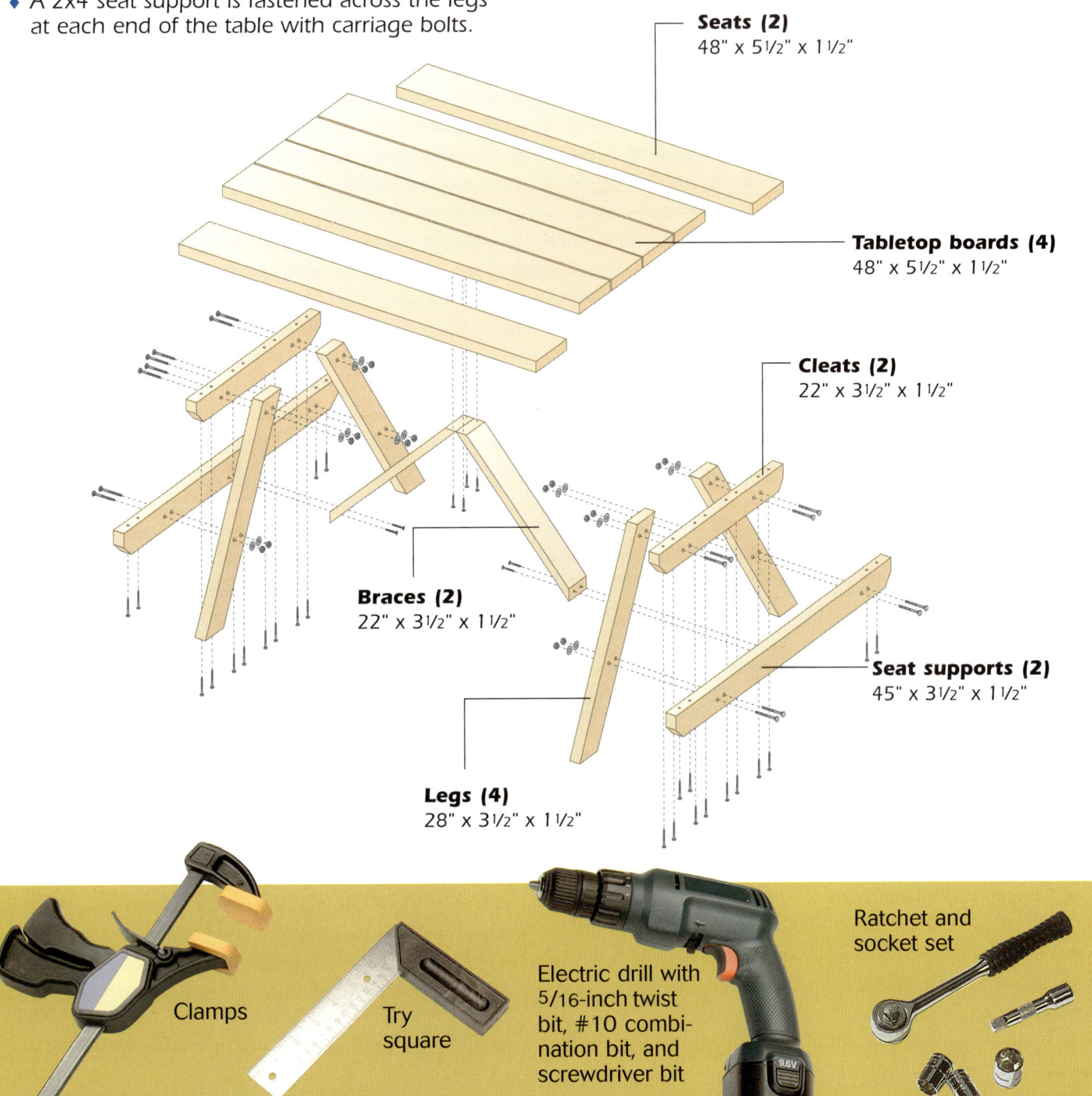

Seats (2)
48" x 5½" x 1½"

Tabletop boards (4)
48" x 5½" x 1½"

Cleats (2)
22" x 3½" x 1½"

Braces (2)
22" x 3½" x 1½"

Seat supports (2)
45" x 3½" x 1½"

Legs (4)
28" x 3½" x 1½"

Clamps

Try square

Electric drill with 5/16-inch twist bit, #10 combination bit, and screwdriver bit

Ratchet and socket set

1 Preparing the tabletop

The tabletop consists of four 2x6 boards spaced ¼ inch apart.

◆ Cut all the pieces of the table to size. Then, set the four tabletop boards on a large work surface such as a workbench or full-sized picnic table.

◆ Place a ¼-inch spacer between each board about 12 inches from each end. (Small pieces of ¼-inch plywood work well.)

◆ With a carpenter's square or straightedge, align the ends of the boards *(left)*.

◆ Clamp the two outside boards to the work surface to prevent the assembly from moving.

1 ½"   1 ½"   1 ½"   1 ½"

Marking and cutting the cleats

A 2x4 cleat holds the tabletop boards together at each end of the table. Their lower corners are trimmed to get rid of sharp edges.

◆ Make two marks 1½ inches from a corner at each end of the cleat *(inset)*.

◆ Connect the two marks with a ruler or a try square *(right)*.

◆ Clamp the cleat to the work surface and trim the corners with a crosscut saw. Mark and trim both corners of the second cleat.

2

Drilling holes in the cleats

You need to drill ½-inch-deep counterbore holes through the cleats so the bottom 1 inch of 4-inch deck screws can pass through the cleat and bite into the tabletop.

◆ With the carpenter's square, mark two lines across the width of the tabletop, each line 7 inches from the end.

◆ Set the cleats across the tabletop, each one even with a marked line. Position the cleats so their ends are set in about ¼ inch from the edges of the tabletop. Mark eight points for screws on the top edge of each cleat, two points per tabletop board. Space the points about 2 inches apart so none is near the edges of the tabletop boards.

◆ Fit your electric drill with a combination bit and adjust it for a ½-inch counterbore hole. Clamp a cleat on edge to the bench, then drill a hole into the cleat at each marked point *(above)*. Repeat for the other cleat.

Attaching the cleats

◆ Reposition a cleat on the tabletop, even with the marked line and ¼ inch from the top's edges.

◆ Drive a 4-inch screw into each hole *(above)*. Make sure the heads of the screws sit at the bottom of the ½-inch-deep counterbore portions of the holes.

◆ Fasten the second cleat at the opposite end of the table, then remove the clamps and spacers.

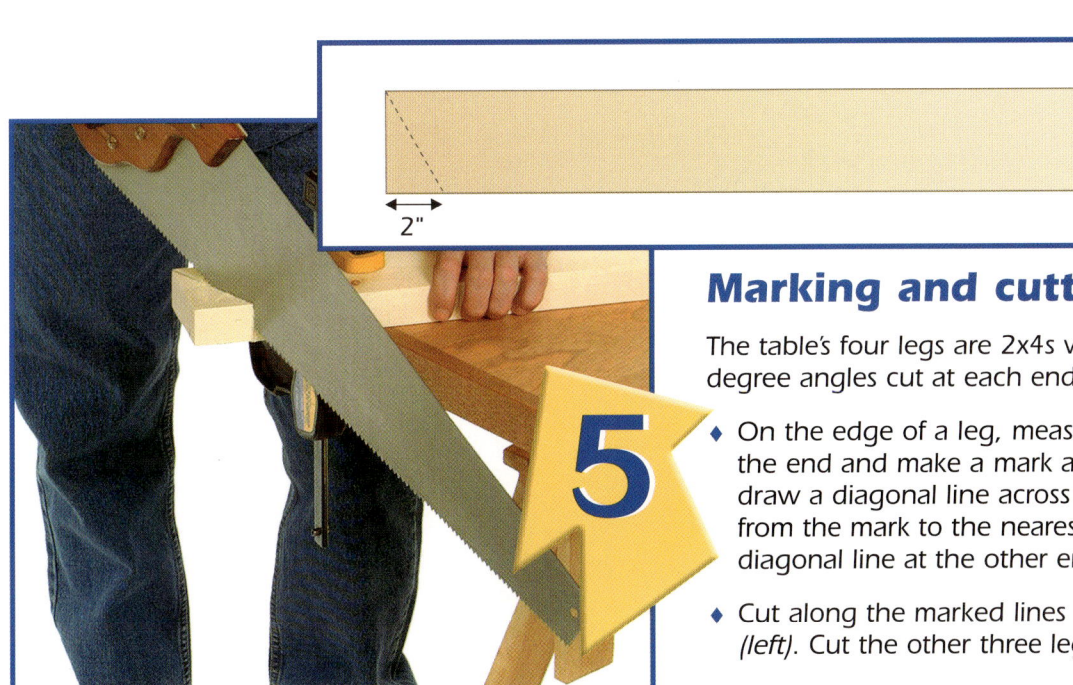

Marking and cutting the legs

The table's four legs are 2x4s with opposing 30-degree angles cut at each end.

◆ On the edge of a leg, measure 2 inches from the end and make a mark at that point. Then, draw a diagonal line across the face of the leg from the mark to the nearest corner. Mark a diagonal line at the other end of the leg *(inset)*.

◆ Cut along the marked lines with a crosscut saw *(left)*. Cut the other three legs this way.

Drilling bolt holes through the legs and cleats

The legs are attached to the cleats with carriage bolts and nuts. Holes for the bolts must be drilled through the legs and cleats.

♦ Position one of the legs flat against a cleat and the tabletop so the end of the leg is centered between the last two tabletop boards. Clamp the leg to the cleat.

♦ Mark two points on the face of the leg 1½ inches up from the end and set in about ¾ inch from each edge of the leg.

♦ Fit a drill with a 5/16-inch bit. With a helper holding the leg steady, drill a hole through the leg and cleat at each mark *(above)*.

Attaching the legs

♦ Slip a carriage bolt into each hole so the head of the bolt sits on the cleat.

♦ Slide a washer over the end of each bolt, then thread a nut onto it. Tighten the nut with a ratchet and socket set *(above)* or a wrench. Repeat steps 6 and 7 to install the other three legs.

Preparing the seat supports

♦ Trim two corners of each seat support as you did in step 2 for the cleats.

♦ Set the supports on the bench with the shorter edges facing up. Mark four points on each support, ½ inch and 2½ inches from each end.

♦ Fit the drill with the combination bit and adjust it for a ½-inch counterbore. Clamp a seat support on edge to the bench, then drill a hole into the support at each marked point *(left)*. Repeat for the other support.

Marking the seat support positions on the legs

◆ Mark a line across the outside face of each leg 14 inches from what will be the bottom end.

◆ Clamp a piece of scrap wood across one leg at each end of the tabletop so the top edge is even with the marked line *(left)*. The boards will help you position and attach the seat supports in steps 10 and 11.

9

Up Close...

Positioning the seat supports

◆ Measuring from one end, mark the center of one seat support. Extend the mark across the board's outside face with a try square.

◆ Set the seat support on the piece of scrap wood on one leg while a helper lines up the support's lower edge with the line on the other leg. Mark the edges of the seat support on both legs to make positioning it easier.

◆ Place a carpenter's square on the tabletop so the outside edge of the square's long arm is centered between the two middle boards of the top. Have your helper position the seat support so the center mark on it lines up with the outside edge of the square *(right)*.

◆ Clamp the seat support to the legs.

10

Align the outside edge of the carpenter's square long arm with the gap between the two middle boards of the tabletop.

Attaching the seat supports

The seat supports are attached to the legs with carriage bolts and nuts.

♦ Mark two points on the face of one leg centered between the edges of the seat support and set in about 3/4 inch from each edge of the leg.

♦ Fit the drill with a 5/16-inch bit and drill a hole through the leg and seat support at each mark *(left)*.

♦ Drill two holes through the second leg and the seat support.

♦ Attach the seat support to the legs with carriage bolts as in step 7 so their heads sit on the outside face of the legs.

♦ Repeat steps 10 and 11 to attach the other seat support to the legs at the opposite end of the table, then remove the clamps.

Adult's Corner...

Marking and cutting the braces

Cutting at an angle through 3 1/2 inches of wood requires precision and a little muscle. The trick is to saw along the marked lines on both the face and edge at the same time.

♦ On the edge of one brace, measure 1 1/2 inches from the end and make a mark at that point.

♦ Draw a diagonal line across the edge from the mark to the opposite corner.

♦ Use a try square to extend the line straight across the face of the board. Mark the other end of the brace this way *(inset)*.

♦ Clamp the brace to the work surface so the diagonal line you marked on the edge is facing up. Make the cut with a crosscut saw *(right)*. Cut the brace at the other end, then saw the other brace.

12

1 1/2"   1 1/2"

Positioning and attaching the braces

♦ Mark the midpoint at each end of one brace, then set it between the tabletop and a seat support so the midpoint at one end aligns with the gap between the two middle boards of the top.

♦ Align the midpoint at the other end of the brace with the center mark on the seat support.

♦ With the ends of the brace flat against the seat support and the tabletop, fasten the brace to the support with a pair of 2½-inch deck screws *(above)*. Center the screws between the edges of the seat support and set in about ¾ inch from each edge of the brace.

♦ Drive two more screws to fasten the other end of the brace to the tabletop. Locate the screws 2 inches from the end of the brace and hold the drill perpendicular to the top— not the braces—as you drive the fasteners.

♦ Attach the other brace to the top and the other seat support the same way.

14

Clamping the seats

♦ Mark a line on the underside of each seat 7 inches from each end. The seats will overhang the support boards by this amount.

♦ With a helper supporting one end of a seat, hold the other end so the line on the seat is even with the outside edge of the seat support. Position the seat board so its outside edge projects beyond the end of the support by about ¼ inch, then clamp the seat to the support *(left)*. Clamp the other end of the seat the same way.

Woodworking Tip

The feet of the picnic table's legs will tend to soak up moisture, especially if they are sitting on wet ground, making them more likely to rot. Protect them with replaceable feet. Cut four ¼-inch-thick pieces of scrap wood, with the grain running lengthwise, 3¾ inches long and 1¼ inches wide. Tack one to the underside of each leg with a pair of ¾-inch galvanized finishing nails *(right)*. If you want, you can even paint, stain, or seal the feet first to match the rest of the table. When they decay, simply pry them off and replace them with new ones.

Attaching the seats

♦ With a screwdriver, drive a 4-inch deck screw through each hole in the seat supports you drilled in step 8 and into the seat *(right)*. Attach the other seat the same way.

♦ Smooth any rough spots or sharp edges on the table with 120-grit sandpaper, then finish it with paint, stain, or water sealer. Pay special attention to any end grain when painting or waterproofing outdoor furniture. The cut ends of boards will suck up a lot more moisture than regular surface wood. Soak them thoroughly, especially the cut ends of the legs.

15

Chapter 3
Great Gifts

Building a Jewelry Box

They say that good things come in small packages, and this jewelry box proves the point. A special place for keeping precious things, this easy-to-build gift will be a big hit with your friends and family.

The cove molding, decorative hasp, and hinges add a touch of class to the box, while a little creative painting can make its own statement. We added flower stickers to our box to give it a sunny, colorful look.

Materials you'll need

Wood	3 feet 1x3 pine
	3 feet 1x1 pine
	10 inches x 6 inches ½-inch plywood
	10 inches x 6 inches ¼-inch tongue-and-groove paneling
	4 feet ½-inch cove molding
Hardware	2 1-inch x 1-inch hinges
	1 metal hasp
Fasteners	#6 1¼-inch screws
	1-inch finishing nails
	1¼-inch finishing nails
Miscellaneous	Wood glue
	Wood filler

The tools you'll need...

Tape measure

Screwdrivers

Try square

Saber saw

Hammer

Crosscut saw

Nail set

How the pieces fit together...

- The back and front are fastened to the sides with counterbored screws, while the sides and ends of the lid frame are glued and nailed together.

- The lid is made of two pieces of tongue-and-groove paneling anchored to the lid frame by glue and nails.

- The plywood base is nailed to the sides, front, and back. Cove molding rings the edges of the base.

- Hinges and a decorative hasp secure the lid to the back and front.

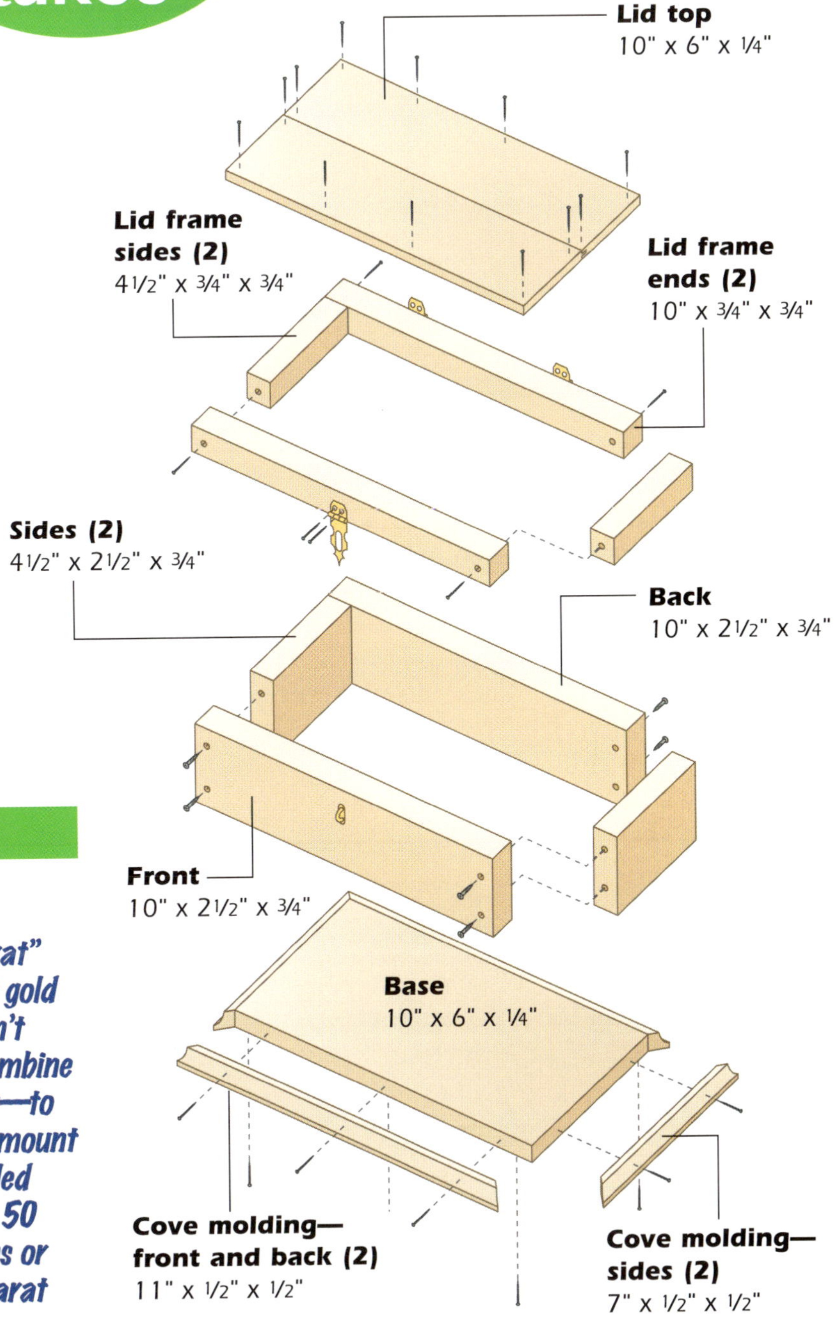

Did You Know...

The Story Behind the Carats in Gold

Did you ever wonder what "14 carat" or "18 carat" on a gold earring or bracelet meant? Well, most gold jewelry is not pure gold. Gold is too soft and won't stand up well to lots of handling. So, jewelers combine gold with other metals—often silver and copper—to make something stronger, called an alloy. The amount of gold in a gold alloy is measured in 24ths, called carats. So, a 12-carat gold alloy is 12/24ths or 50 percent gold, an 18-carat gold alloy is 18/24ths or 75 percent gold. A piece of jewelry that is 24 carat is pure gold—and usually quite expensive!

Lid top
10" x 6" x 1/4"

Lid frame sides (2)
4 1/2" x 3/4" x 3/4"

Lid frame ends (2)
10" x 3/4" x 3/4"

Sides (2)
4 1/2" x 2 1/2" x 3/4"

Back
10" x 2 1/2" x 3/4"

Front
10" x 2 1/2" x 3/4"

Base
10" x 6" x 1/4"

Cove molding—front and back (2)
11" x 1/2" x 1/2"

Cove molding—sides (2)
7" x 1/2" x 1/2"

Clamp

Miter box

Electric drill with 7/32-inch twist bit, #6 combination bit, and screwdriver bit

Sanding block and 80- and 120-grit sandpaper

Backsaw

Straightedge

1

Marking pilot holes in the front, back, and sides

♦ Cut the front, back, and sides and the pieces of the lid to size.

♦ With a try square, mark a line 1/2 inch from the ends of the back and front.

♦ Mark two points on each line, 1/2 inch from the edges of the piece *(left)*.

2

Fastening the front, back, and sides

♦ Assemble the sides, front, and back on a worktable, securing the pieces together with clamps. Make sure the ends of the front and back are flush with the outside faces of the sides.

♦ Fit your electric drill with a combination bit and adjust it for a 1/4-inch counterbore. Drill holes into the front and back at the marks.

♦ Drive a screw into each hole *(left)*.

Cutting the base

You can have the base cut to size at the lumberyard or do it yourself, as described here.

♦ Lay the box on a piece of plywood, lining up two sides of the box with two sides of the plywood. With a pencil, trace the outline of the other two sides of the box on the plywood *(left)*.

♦ Clamp the plywood to the table with one of the marked lines overhanging the edge, then cut along the line with a backsaw.

♦ Cut along the other line.

Woodworking Tip

A quick, handy way to draw a line near the edge of a piece of wood is the old carpenter's trick of using your hand as a guide. Holding a pencil so the tip extends from your fingers by the amount you want, keep the tips of your fingers pressed tightly against the edge of the wood as you draw your hand down the piece of wood (left).

Fastening the base

♦ Mark lines 3/8 inch from the ends and edges of the base. Mark a point at each corner where the lines meet and at the midpoint of each line.

♦ Set the box upside down on the table and apply a narrow bead of glue along its edges. Clamp the base on top so its ends and edges are flush with the box.

♦ Drive a 1-inch finishing nail through the base at each marked point *(right)*.

5

Assembling the lid frame

♦ Place the sides of the lid frame on end on the worktable. Position one of the end pieces across them so the corners of the three pieces are perfectly aligned.

♦ With a helper holding the pieces in position, use a hammer to tap a 1¼-inch finishing nail through the end piece into the side *(left)*.

♦ Fasten the end piece to the other side, then turn over the pieces and nail the opposite end piece in place.

Preparing the lid top

To make the two tongue-and-groove pieces of the box lid fit exactly over the lid frame, the tongue of one piece must be sanded off the edge.

♦ Clamp one of the panel pieces to the worktable with its tongue overhanging the table edge.

♦ Fit a sanding block with 80-grit paper. Working in smooth, downward strokes, sand the tongue until it is flush with the edge of the panel *(right)*.

6

Assembling the lid

♦ Run a bead of wood glue along both sides of the tongue of the panel piece you didn't sand.

♦ Holding the two panel pieces flat on the work-table, slide the glued tongue into the groove of the other piece *(right)*, locking the two pieces tightly together.

♦ Clamp the top on the lid frame so its ends and edges are flush with the frame. Draw lines 3/8 inch from the ends and edges of the top, then mark a point at each corner of the panel pieces along the lines.

♦ Drive a 1¼-inch finishing nail through the top at each marked point to fasten it to the frame.

Adult's Corner...

Beveling the edges of the lid

The sharp top edges of the box lid are flattened, or beveled, to give the box a more finished look.

♦ Clamp the lid to the worktable so one side overhangs the edge.

♦ Flatten the sharp edge of the lid by passing the sanding block along it at a 60-degree angle.

♦ Bevel the other three edges of the lid the same way *(right)*.

9

Cutting the cove molding

♦ Cut one end of a piece of cove molding at a 45-degree angle with a backsaw and a miter box.

♦ Position the molding against the jewelry box, aligning the cut end with one of the box corners. Mark the molding where it meets the adjoining corner. Miter the molding at the mark, cutting a 45-degree angle opposite to the first *(left)*.

♦ Cut the other molding pieces in the same way. To help you position the molding on the box, label the sides of the box and the molding pieces that go with them A, B, C, and D as you cut the pieces.

10

Attaching the molding to the base

♦ On the outside face of the pieces of cove molding, measure and mark a point 2½ inches from each end.

♦ Tap a 1-inch finishing nail into the molding pieces at each mark.

♦ Place the box on one side on the worktable. Run a bead of glue on the inside face of one of the molding pieces, position it on the box, then gently drive the nails to secure the molding in place *(right)*.

♦ Fasten the remaining pieces of molding the same way.

Fastening the hinges

♦ Position the lid on the box, lining up the edges. Clamp the two pieces together and set the box on its front on the worktable.

♦ Mark lines across the seam between the lid and the back 1½ inches from each edge of the box.

♦ Line up the outside edges of the hinges with the lines, centering the hinge pins on the seam.

♦ Fasten the hinges to the box with the nails provided *(right)*.

Attaching the hasp

♦ Turn the box over on its back and place it on two pieces of scrap wood to raise the hinges off the worktable.

♦ Measure along the seam between the lid and the front, and mark the midpoint with a line.

♦ Center the hasp with the line, then disengage the strap from the staple and fasten the staple to the front of the box with the nails provided.

♦ Engage the strap with the staple and fasten it to the lid of the box *(left)*.

♦ Sink all the nail heads below the surface of the wood with a nail set and a hammer.

♦ Fill all the nail holes with wood filler. Let the filler dry, then sand the surface with 120-grit sandpaper.

Personalizing Your Jewelry Box

You can protect the valuables in your jewelry box and add a neat decorative touch at the same time by covering the bottom with felt. Felt is available at most fabric stores. Cut the felt into strips to cover the bottom and inner sides of the box and the underside of the lid. Spread a thin layer of glue on these surfaces of the box and press the felt into place. Now, just let the glue dry and you're ready to load up your jewelry box with your favorite possessions.

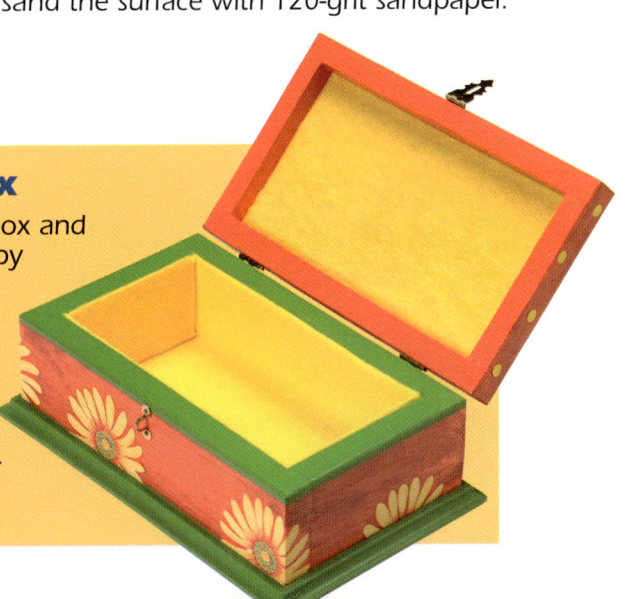

Building a # Kitchen Trivet

Got something too hot to handle? This kitchen trivet gives you a place to set it down! Featuring a wooden frame built around a single ceramic tile, this simple-to-make gift is a handy and decorative addition to any kitchen.

The trivet is made with a tile 8 inches square—the perfect size for items such as a kettle or casserole dish. Choose a glazed tile for easy cleanups, and add self-adhesive cork pads so the trivet doesn't slip. As for color and style, you'll find the variety of tiles out there about as wide as your imagination, so be creative!

Materials you'll need

Wood	4 feet 1x2 pine
	12 inches x 12 inches
	¾-inch particleboard
Fasteners	1-inch finishing nails
	1¼-inch finishing nails
Miscellaneous	Wood glue
	Latex-based adhesive caulk
	8-inch-square ceramic tile
	4 adhesive cork pads
	Wood filler

The tools you'll need...

Tape measure

Miter box

Crosscut saw

Try square

Backsaw

How the pieces fit together...

- The frame pieces are glued and nailed to the edges of the 3/4-inch particleboard base.

- The corners of the frame are reinforced with finishing nails.

- The tile is secured to the base with adhesive caulk.

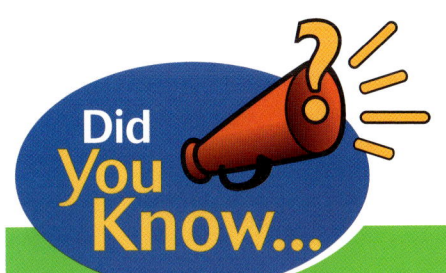

Did You Know...

How Tiles Were Invented

Tiles first appeared about 6,000 years ago in Egypt, when wet clay was gathered from riverbeds, set in square frames, and dried in the sun. These tiles got a boost when someone tried putting them in the oven with the bread! When tiles were baked or "fired," they became much more waterproof and lasted longer. The use of colored glazes led to another chance discovery. These natural pigments protected the surface, and made the tiles one of the first items used in home decoration—that is, after cave paintings!

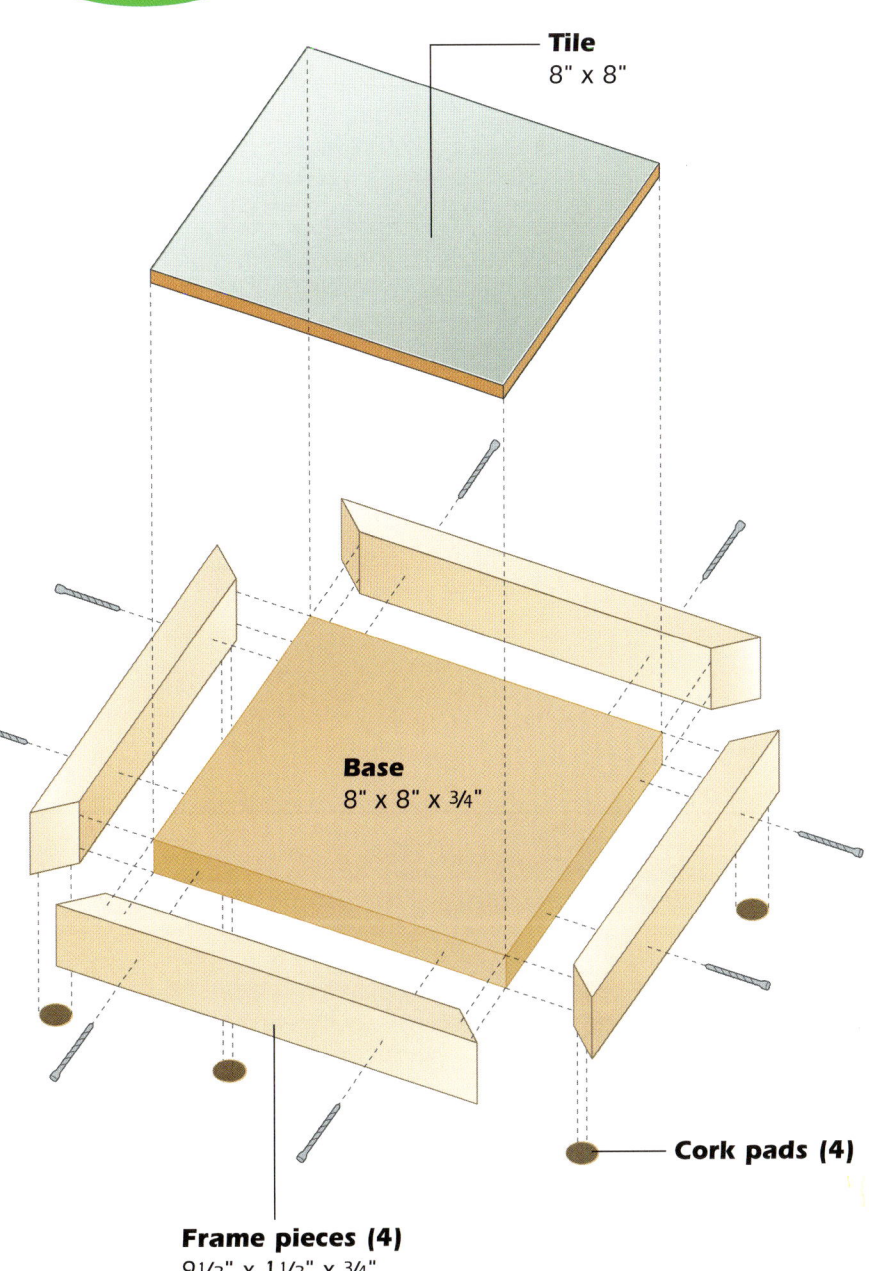

Tile
8" x 8"

Base
8" x 8" x 3/4"

Frame pieces (4)
9 1/2" x 1 1/2" x 3/4"

Cork pads (4)

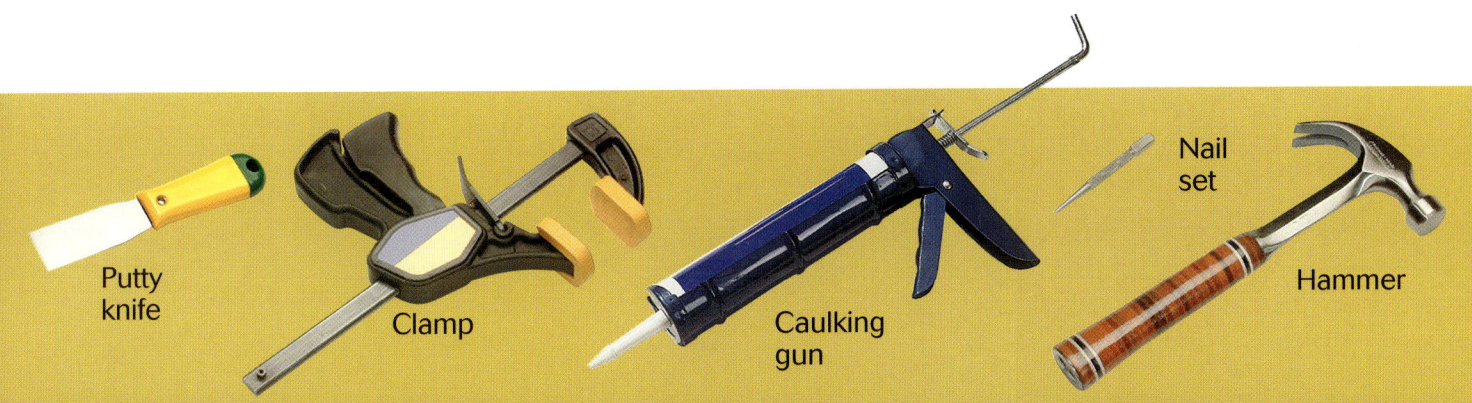

Putty knife

Clamp

Caulking gun

Nail set

Hammer

Marking the size of the base

Even though a tile may be marked 8 inches x 8 inches, the exact size may be slightly different. To make sure the base will be exactly the same size as the tile, outline the tile on the particleboard before cutting it to size.

♦ Lay the tile on the particleboard base, lining up two sides of the tile with two sides of the base. With a pencil, trace the outline of the other two sides of the tile on the base *(right)*. Stick a strip of masking tape on each edge of the tile. Label the strips and the edges of the base that go with them A, B, C, and D.

♦ Clamp the base to the table with one of the marked lines overhanging the edge, then cut along the line with a crosscut saw. Cut along the other line.

Marking the frame

♦ Place a frame piece on edge in a miter box and cut one end at a 45-degree angle with a backsaw. Clamp the frame piece to the miter box for extra stability.

♦ Position the piece against the edge of the base labeled A, aligning the cut end with one of the base's corners. Mark the piece where it meets the adjoining corner *(left)*.

Cutting the frame

- Miter the frame piece at the mark, cutting a 45-degree angle opposite the first *(right)*. Label the piece A.

- Cut and label the other molding pieces in the same way.

3

Woodworking Tip

On your mark! Cutting frame pieces so the corners fit snugly depends on accuracy. Saw just outside your mark. Cutting inside the mark or way outside it can create gaps later on, so take your time and keep an eye on where the blade is touching the workpiece.

4

Marking the tile height on the frame

The tile should sit flush with the top edges of the frame. Marking a reference line on the inside of the frame before assembly will help make this happen.

- Lay the tile face down on the work surface and hold the inside face of a frame piece against the edge of the tile.

- Draw a pencil line along the tile to mark a reference line on the frame piece *(left)*. Mark the other three frame pieces the same way.

Marking the nail locations

- On the outside face of each frame piece, measure and mark two points 1 inch from the bottom edge. Join the marks, drawing a light pencil line along the length of the frame with a straightedge.

- Mark two points along each line, 2 inches from each end *(right)*.

5

Fastening the frame

Driving the nails partway through the frame pieces before fastening them to the base will free up your hands during assembly and enable you to hold the pieces steady.

♦ Set one of the frame pieces inside-face down on a piece of scrap wood on the worktable.

♦ Drive a 1¼-inch finishing nail into the piece at each marked point until the tip of the nail just breaks the surface of the other side. Drive nails into the other frame pieces this way.

♦ Place the base on the table with the edge labeled A facing up.

♦ Run a bead of glue along the inside face of the frame piece marked A, then position it on the base, lining up the reference line you marked in step 4 with the top surface of the base.

♦ Drive the nails in the frame piece all the way *(right)*, anchoring the piece to the base. Fasten the other frame pieces to the base.

6

7

Nailing the corners

To give the trivet frame extra strength, drive a nail into each corner.

♦ With the trivet on edge, hammer a 1-inch finishing nail into the frame piece ¾ inch from the corner. Angle the nail slightly toward the outside edge *(left)*.

♦ Drive a nail into the other three corners the same way.

♦ Sink all the nail heads below the surface with a nail set and a hammer.

8

Applying the adhesive

♦ Set the base face up on the worktable.

♦ Starting near the top left corner of the base, lay a continuous bead of nontoxic, latex-based adhesive caulk around and across the surface *(left)*.

9

Anchoring the tile

♦ Position the tile on the base so the edge labeled A sits against the corresponding frame piece *(right)*.

♦ Press down on the tile to make good contact with the base.

10

Finishing touches

♦ With a putty knife, cover the nail holes with a dab of wood filler. Let the filler dry, then sand it smooth.

♦ Paint or varnish the frame.

♦ Affix an adhesive cork pad to each corner on the underside of the frame *(left)*.

Building a Recipe Box

Tired of hunting around for that wonderful recipe written on a scrap of paper and lost in a drawer? This recipe box solves the problem and makes a handy and decorative kitchen gift!

The box is just the right size for 4x6 recipe cards, and with a hook fastened to the arched back panel, it can be hung on a wall close in the kitchen. As you'll see in the list of materials, the only wood you need for this project are a few short pieces—a chance to give new life to those cutoffs you thought you'd never use!

Materials you'll need

Wood	12 inches 1x10 pine
	12 inches 1x6 pine
	12 inches 1x5 pine
	2 feet 1x4 pine
Hardware	2 cotter pin hinges
	Metal hook
Fasteners	#6 1¼-inch screws
Miscellaneous	Wood glue
	Wood plugs for #6 screws

The tools you'll need...

Try square

Compass

Screwdrivers

Tape measure

Sanding block and 120-grit sandpaper

Crosscut saw

How the pieces fit together...

- The sides, bottom, front, and back are all fastened together with screws.
- Wood plugs conceal the screws in the front.
- Cotter pins hinge the flip-top lid to the back panel.

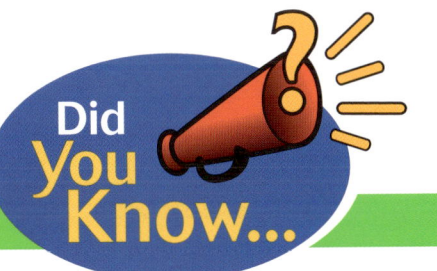

How to Make Chocolate Chip Cookies

*1/2 pound butter
1 cup brown sugar
3/4 cup white sugar
2 eggs
1 tsp vanilla extract
2 cups all-purpose flour
1 tsp baking soda
1 tsp salt
1 1/2 cups semisweet chocolate chips*

Preheat your oven to 350°F. Melt the butter, adding both types of sugar. Beat in the eggs and vanilla. Sift the dry ingredients, then add them to the butter and eggs. Add the chocolate chips last. With a spoon, form the batter into cookie shapes and space them out on a greased cookie sheet. Bake for 8 to 10 minutes until brown. This recipe makes about two dozen cookies.

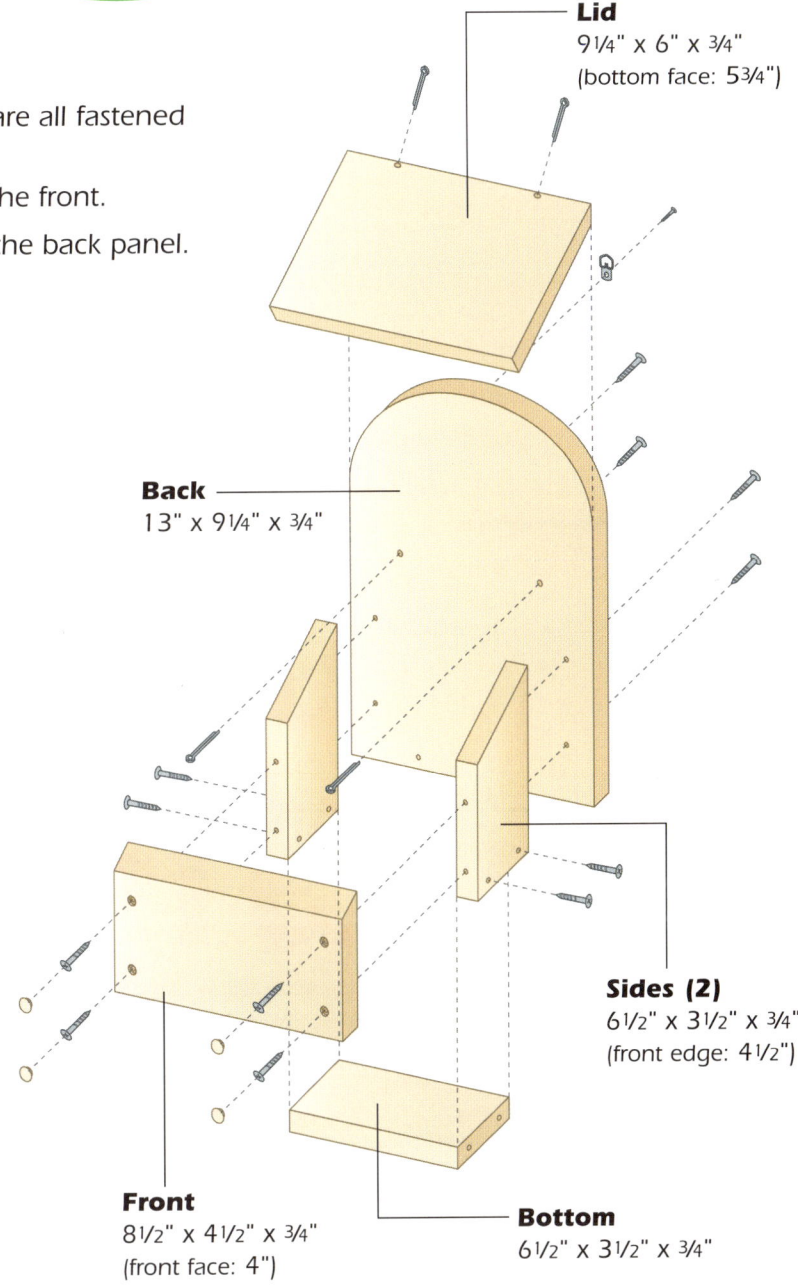

Lid
9 1/4" x 6" x 3/4"
(bottom face: 5 3/4")

Back
13" x 9 1/4" x 3/4"

Sides (2)
6 1/2" x 3 1/2" x 3/4"
(front edge: 4 1/2")

Front
8 1/2" x 4 1/2" x 3/4"
(front face: 4")

Bottom
6 1/2" x 3 1/2" x 3/4"

Long-nose pliers

Straightedge

Clamps

Plane

Saber saw

Electric drill with 1/8-inch twist bit and #6 combination bit

1 Marking the arch of the back

Two arcs drawn from each side and meeting at the top form a cutting line for sawing the arch in the back of the recipe box.

♦ Cut the back piece of the box to length.

♦ With a try square, draw a horizontal line across the face of the back piece 3¼ inches from the top. Draw two vertical lines 3¼ inches from each edge.

♦ Set the point of a compass at one of the spots where the lines cross and extend the pencil to the nearest edge of the piece. Scribe an arc that contacts the edge and top of the piece.

♦ Reposition the compass at the second point where the lines cross and draw an arc at the other corner *(left)*.

Adult's Corner...

Cutting the arch

2

Making a smooth, accurate curved cut with a saber saw takes a little practice—even for an adult. Don't rush your cut: Work slowly to keep the blade on line.

♦ Clamp the back piece to your worktable so the marked curve overhangs the edge.

♦ With a saber saw, cut the arcs, following the marked lines *(right)*.

3

Marking the angles of the sides

The angled tops of both side pieces can be made with a single cut on a 1x4.

◆ Measuring from one end of a 1x4, mark one point 6 1/2 inches along one edge and another point 4 1/2 inches along the other *(left)*.

◆ Join the points with a straightedge.

Woodworking Tip

When cutting more than one piece from a board, it's best to measure and mark after each cut, rather than marking all the cuts at the start. The width of each cut—the kerf—will eat up 1/4 inch of wood, making every piece too short.

Cutting the side and bottom pieces

4

◆ Clamp the 1x4 to the worktable with the marked line overhanging and parallel to the table's edge.

◆ Cut along the mark with a crosscut saw *(right)*—that takes care of one side piece.

◆ Mark a cutting line for the other side piece by measuring from the cut end 4 1/2 inches along the shorter edge of what's left of the 1x4. With a try square, mark the line across the piece from this point to the opposite edge.

◆ Reposition the 1x4 on the table and cut along the line.

◆ Measure and mark another line 6 1/2 inches from the last cut. Sawing along the line will yield the bottom piece.

5

Fastening the bottom and sides

◆ With a try square, mark a line across the outside face of each side piece 3/8 inch from the bottom edge. On each line, mark a point 3/4 inch from each edge.

◆ Run a bead of glue along the ends of the bottom piece, then clamp the bottom between the sides, making sure the bottom is flush with the straight ends of the sides. Clamp the boards to the table.

◆ Fit a drill with a combination bit and drill a countersink hole at each mark *(left)*. Drive a screw into each hole.

Fastening the back piece

6

♦ With a try square, mark two vertical lines on the outside face of the back 1 inch from each edge. Mark a horizontal line across the piece 3/8 inch from the bottom.

♦ Mark two points along each vertical line 2 and 5 inches from the bottom, and two points along the horizontal line 2¼ inches from each edge.

♦ To help position the sides on the back piece, mark two points on the inside face of the back ½ inch from each edge. Place the back piece face up on the worktable.

♦ Run a bead of glue along the back edges of the sides and bottom. Position the sides between the two marks on the back, making sure their bottom edges are flush with the bottom of the back piece.

♦ Turn over the assembly and clamp it to the worktable. Drill a countersink hole at each mark on the back piece and drive a screw into each hole *(right)*.

7

Marking the angled top edge of the front piece

For the recipe box lid to sit flush on the sides and front, the top edge of the front piece must be trimmed to the same angle as the sides.

♦ Cut the front piece to length.

♦ Lay the box on its back and position the front piece on the sides, its bottom edge flush with the bottom of the box.

♦ Align a straightedge with the top edge of one side and run a pencil along it to mark the angle on the end of the front piece *(left)*. Mark the angle on the other end of the front piece, then draw a line across the face of the board to join the two marks.

Adult's Corner...

Planing the angle

Planing at an angle takes some practice. You must keep the plane tilted at the right angle and guide it with long, even strokes. If the plane digs into the wood, lessen the cutting depth with the round adjustment knob to peel thin shavings.

8

◆ Clamp the front piece to the worktable with the marked line overhanging the table's edge.

◆ Holding the plane at the same angle as the mark on the ends of the piece, slide the tool along the full length of the corner. Continue planing *(right)* until you cut to the marks on the board.

Fastening the front

9

◆ Mark two vertical lines on the front piece 5/8 inch from each edge. Mark two points along each line 1 inch and 3¼ inches from the bottom.

◆ Set the box on its back, then center the front piece on the sides, its bottom edge even with the bottom of the box. Clamp the front in place. Adjust the combination bit on your drill for a counterbore hole of the same depth as the wood plugs you'll be using. Drill a hole into the front piece at each point *(right)*.

◆ Drive a screw into each hole, making sure the heads of the screws sit at the bottom of the counterbore portions of the holes.

10 Angling the back edge of the lid

For the back edge of the lid to sit flush against the back piece, it must be planed to the same angle as the sides.

♦ Cut the lid to length. Set the box on its back and hold the lid against one side so one edge of the lid is even with the top end of the side.

♦ Run a pencil along the top of the side piece to mark the angle on the end of the lid *(left)*. Mark the angle on the other end of the lid, then draw a line across the face of the lid to join the two marks.

♦ Plane the edge of the lid as you did the front piece in step 8.

Drilling holes in the back piece for the cotter pin hinges

♦ Position the lid on the sides with the planed edge flush against the back piece.

♦ Mark two points along the edge of the lid 2 inches from the end. Mark two points on the back piece in line with the marks on the lid and just above them. Set the lid aside.

♦ Clamp the box on its back on top of a scrap board on the worktable.

♦ Fit the drill with a 1/8-inch bit, then drill a hole through the back piece at each mark *(right)*.

11

12

Drilling holes in the lid

♦ Clamp the lid on top of the scrap piece on the worktable.

♦ Holding the drill at the same angle as the edge of the lid, drill through the lid at each mark *(left)*.

Installing the hinges

♦ Slide a cotter pin into each hole in the top of the lid.

♦ With long-nose pliers, bend the ends of the pins flat against the underside of the lid *(right)*, making sure the loops are tight against the top of the lid.

13

Hinging the lid to the box

♦ Engage a cotter pin with each one on the lid, hooking the ends through the loops.

♦ Slide the ends of the pins into the holes in the front of the back piece *(left)*.

♦ Bend the ends of the pins flat against the back of the box.

♦ Fasten a metal hook to the outside face of the back piece with the screw provided, making sure to center the hook between the edges.

14

Finishing touches

♦ Dab wood glue on the ends of the wood plugs and push them into the screw holes on the front of the box *(right)*.

♦ Sand all the edges of the box with 120-grit sandpaper.

♦ Finish and decorate the box with stain, paint, or stencils.

15

Building a Spice Rack

A great gift for anyone who spends time in the kitchen, this double-shelf spice rack can hold more than two dozen spice bottles of varying heights.

In this project, you'll learn a neat way to draw and cut a curve, and drill holes for wood plugs. The shelf rails, made from dowels, slide in and out so adding or removing bottles is a snap.

Materials you'll need

Wood	2 feet 1x8 pine
	4 feet 1x3 pine
	12 inches 1x4 pine
	4 feet 3⁄8-inch dowel
Hardware	2 metal hooks
Fasteners	#6 1¼-inch screws
	1-inch spiral finishing nails
Miscellaneous	Wood glue
	Wood plugs for #6 screws
	Wood filler

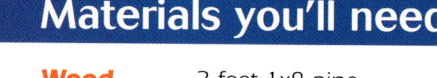

The tools you'll need...

Hammer

Screwdrivers

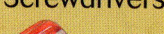
Tape measure

Nail set

Try square

Crosscut saw

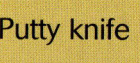
Putty knife

Shelf rails (2)
24" x 3/8"

Back
22" x 7¼" x ¾"

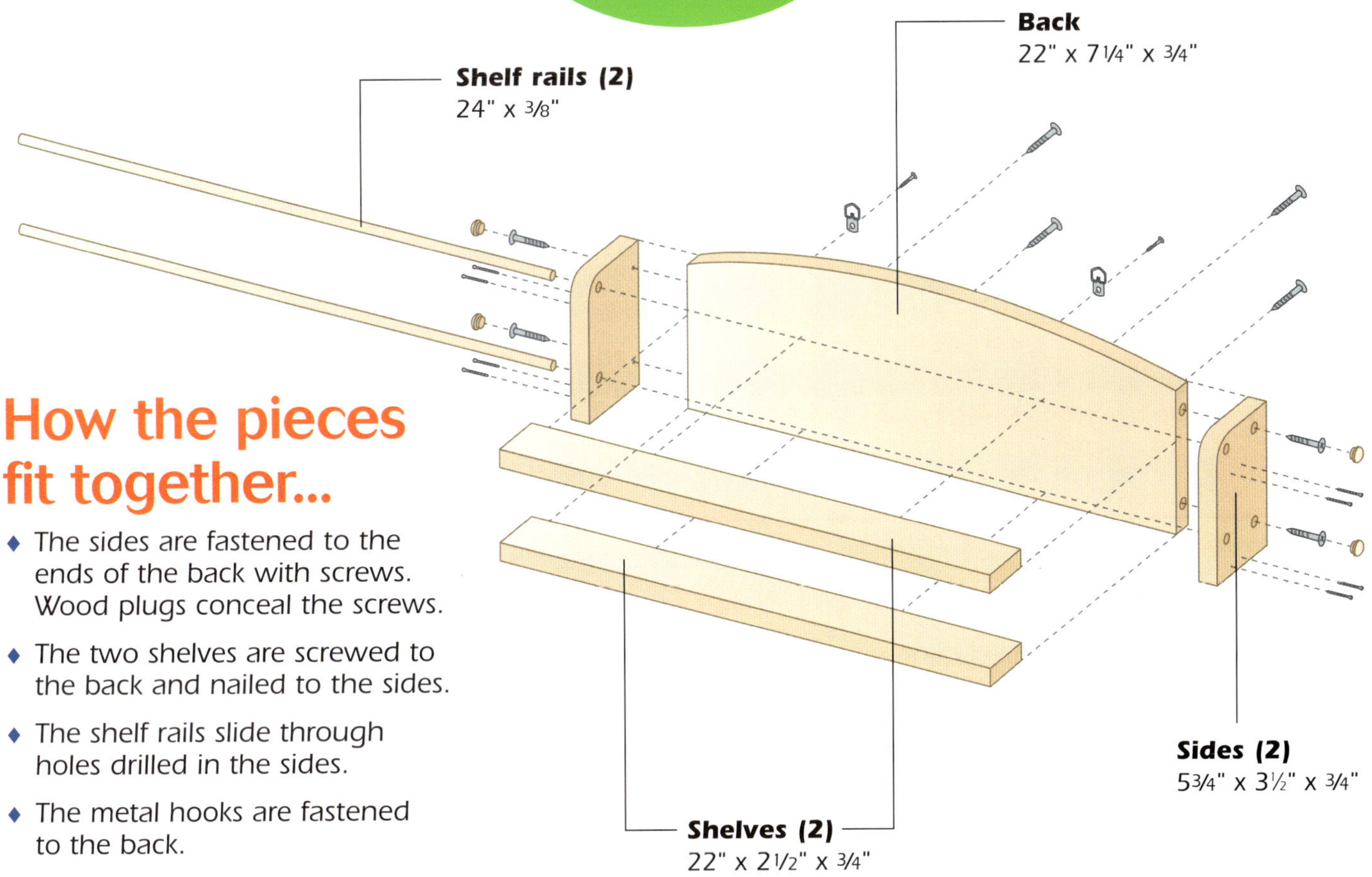

How the pieces fit together...

◆ The sides are fastened to the ends of the back with screws. Wood plugs conceal the screws.

◆ The two shelves are screwed to the back and nailed to the sides.

◆ The shelf rails slide through holes drilled in the sides.

◆ The metal hooks are fastened to the back.

Sides (2)
5¾" x 3½" x ¾"

Shelves (2)
22" x 2½" x ¾"

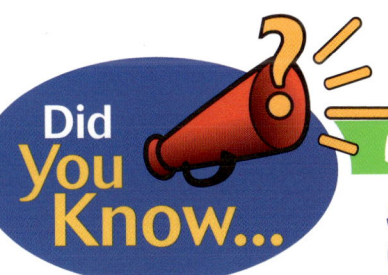
Did You Know...

Where Spices Come From

Spices were once thought to have miraculous properties and were highly valued. They were so rare that explorers were sent off in search of them and to discover the best routes for trading. In looking for these trade routes, explorers discovered America and the West Indies. Eventually, traders went all the way to the Far East in search of spices. Today only saffron is considered a very precious spice. To produce just one pound of saffron, it takes more than a quarter million saffron flower stigmas—each one collected by hand!

Clamps

Saber saw

Sanding block and 120-grit sandpaper

Rasp

Electric drill with 3/8-inch spade bit and #6 combination bit

Cutting the pieces

- On a 1x8, measure and mark a length of 22 inches for the back panel.

- Clamp the piece to your worktable with the cutting line overhanging the edge.

- With a crosscut saw, cut along the line *(left)*.

- Cut the shelves—also to 22 inches—from a 1x3 and the sides to 5¾ inches from a 1x4.

Marking the curve for the back panel

There are several ways to mark a curve. For the method shown here, all you need is a tape measure, a pencil, and a thin, flexible wood strip such as a wooden yardstick.

- Clamp the back to the table, then measure and mark the midpoint of the top edge. Also measure and mark a point at each end 2¼ inches from the top edge.

- With both hands, hold the wood strip on edge on the back panel so the middle of the strip aligns with the midpoint of the panel. Keeping the strip on the midpoint, gently flex the ends toward you until they both touch the points along the edges.

- With the wood strip held steady, run a pencil along it to mark the curve on the panel *(right)*.

Adult's Corner...

Cutting the curve

Following a curve with a saber saw takes a practiced eye. Don't rush—going slowly will make it easier to stay on line.

3

- Clamp the back panel so the marked line overhangs the edge of the table. Position the clamps so they won't interfere with the saw.

- Feed the blade into the panel at one end of the marked curve. Guide the saw slowly along the line *(right)*. When you reach the top of the curve, stop the saw. Reposition the panel so you can finish the cut from the opposite end of the curve. Remember to keep the power cord draped over your shoulder as you saw.

Marking the screw holes on the back

The screws that anchor the shelves to the back require countersink holes so the screws heads can sit flush.

- Along the bottom edge of the back panel, measure and mark points 5 inches from each end.

- With a try square, draw a line upward from each mark, perpendicular to the bottom edge.

- Make two marks along each line, 3/8 inch and 4 inches from the bottom *(right)*.

4

5

Marking the dowel holes on the sides

- With a pencil and try square, draw a vertical line 1/2 inch from the front edge of one side.

- Measure and mark two points along the line, 5/8 inch from the top and 1 3/8 inches from the bottom *(left)*.

- Mark the dowel holes on the other side.

Drilling the dowel holes

6

- Clamp one of the sides on a piece of scrap wood to the worktable.

- Fit a drill with a 3/8-inch spade bit and drill through the side at each mark *(right)*.

- Repeat for the other side.

- Mark L on what will be the inside of the left panel and R on what will be the inside of the right panel.

7

Rounding the top front corners of the sides

- Use a soup can to scribe an arc at the top front corner of one of the sides by lining up the rim of the can with the edges of the piece. Make sure the mark clears the dowel hole by at least 1/2 inch. If not, try with a smaller can.

- Clamp the side to the table with the marked corner facing up.

- Round over the corner with a rasp *(left)* or use a saber saw to make the cut. Either way, remove wood up to your marked line.

- Round over the corner of the other side piece the same way.

Screws

3/8"

1" 3⁵/8" 1"

Nails

2¼"

3/4"

Dowels 3/8"

Preparing the sides for assembly

◆ Referring to the inset illustration, measure and mark points for two screws and four nails on the outside face of one side *(left)*. The screws secure the back and the nails hold the shelves. Mark points on the other side piece the same way.

8

Assembling the rack

◆ Measure and mark a line across the inside of each side panel, 3⁵/8 inches from the bottom. The upper shelf will sit at this line.

◆ Run a bead of wood glue along the ends of the back. Position the sides against the back, making sure the bottoms of the pieces are flush and the back edge of the sides are even with the outside face of the back.

◆ Spread some glue on the ends of the shelves and position them against the back and sides. Line up the underside of the lower shelf with the bottom of the sides and the underside of the upper shelf with the line on the sides.

◆ With a helper keeping the pieces aligned, secure the pieces together with a long clamp *(right)*.

9

Fastening the sides to the back

- Clamp the rack to the table, then fit a combination bit in the drill. Adjust the bit for a counterbore hole of the same depth as the wood plugs you'll be using. Drill a hole into the sides at each marked screw point *(left)*.

- Drive a screw into each hole, making sure the heads of the screws sit at the bottom of the counterbore portions of the holes.

Fastening the shelves

- Drill a countersink hole into the back panel at each marked point.

- Drive a screw into each hole *(right)*.

Nailing the shelves to the sides

For extra strength, spiral finishing nails fix the shelves to the sides.

- Set the spice rack on one side and drive a finishing nail into the opposite side at each marked point you made in step 8 *(left)*.

- Turn over the rack and drive in the nails on the other side.

- Sink the nail heads with a nail set and the hammer.

- Trim the dowels to 22¼ inches and insert them into their holes, leaving ⅛ inch projecting from each side.

A Sticky Story

There are lots of adhesives on the market—stuff such as contact cement, epoxy, and glue with long names like cyanoacrylate and polyvinyl acetate. Years ago adhesives were made from natural materials such as animal hide, fish, and even blood. Today they tend to be chemical-based. For most woodworking projects—and for all the ones in this book—the best type to buy is the yellow carpenter's glue that is available at most hardware stores. It is inexpensive, dries reasonably quickly, can be sanded, and is strong. If you spill any glue on your project, wipe it off with a damp cloth. It's a lot easier than trying to remove blobs of dried glue from your finished masterpiece.

Finishing touches

- Place the spice rack face down on the table. Fasten two metal hooks to the outside face of the back with the screws provided, 4 inches from each end and ⅜ inch from the top edge.

- Dab wood glue on the ends of the wood plugs *(right)* and push them into the screw holes on the sides of the rack.

- Fill all the nail holes with wood filler and let it dry. Sand the rack with 120-grit sandpaper, removing any pencil lines that will show, and finish it with two coats of wood varnish.

Building a # Spaghetti Measure

For any cook who has made more spaghetti than his or her guests can eat—or worse, not enough—this easy project is a real lifesaver.

The way it works is simple. The amount of uncooked spaghetti you can fit through the holes will be enough for one, two, three, or four portions. Because maple is more durable and less porous than pine or spruce, we used it for our spaghetti measure, but any hardwood will do. Bon appetit!

Materials you'll need

Wood	15 inches x 4 inches ½-inch maple
Miscellaneous	Leather strip (for hanging)

The tools you'll need...

Sanding block and 120-grit sandpaper

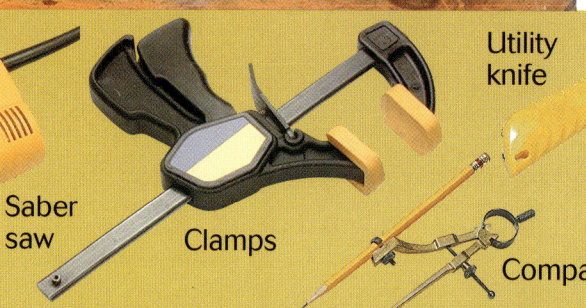

Saber saw

Clamps

Utility knife

Compass

Electric drill with ¼-inch twist bit, 7/8-, 1 3/8-, and 1 ½-inch spade bits, and 1 3/4-inch hole saw

How to cut the piece...

♦ Use the pattern at right to trace the shape and mark the holes of your spaghetti measure. Enlarge the pattern (200 percent) so it is 10 1/2 inches long. The diameter of the holes should be—from biggest to smallest—1 3/4, 1 1/2, and 1 3/8 inches and 7/8 inch.

♦ The shape is cut with a saber saw. The holes are drilled with a hole saw and spade bits; the hanging hole is drilled with a 1/4-inch twist bit.

Did You Know...

The History of Spaghetti

There is a tale that in the 13th century Italian explorer Marco Polo brought the first spaghetti (and other pasta) back to Italy from China. It's a good story, but there's one problem: It isn't true. Ancient records show the first dried pasta appeared with the rise of the Roman Empire 2,000 years ago, long before Marco Polo went to China. The real story is that as the population of Rome grew bigger and bigger, there weren't enough places to store all the grain that people needed. Someone soon discovered a new recipe that involved grinding the grain into flour, mixing it with eggs to make a dough, cutting it into strips, and drying it in the sun. The result? Pasta, a handy, healthy food that took up less space and could keep well for more than a year.

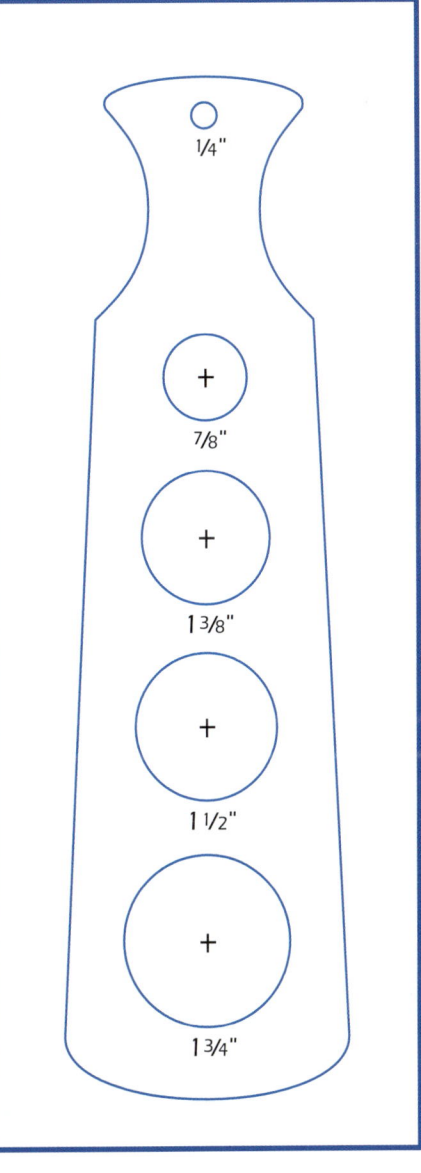

1/4"

+
7/8"

+
1 3/8"

+
1 1/2"

+
1 3/4"

1 Tracing the shape

◆ Enlarge the pattern on page 131 so it is 10½ inches long (a 200 percent enlargement).

◆ With a utility knife or scissors, cut out the shape.

◆ Lay the cutout flat against your piece of wood. Tape or hold it in place and trace the shape on the surface *(left)*.

Marking the holes

◆ With the pattern still in place, push the point of a compass into the center point of each circle to mark its location. Set the pattern aside.

◆ Adjust the compass to the radius of the largest hole: ⁷/₈ inch (which is half the diameter). Then, set the compass point at the center mark you made on the wood for the largest hole and draw the circle *(right)*.

◆ Draw circles for the other spaghetti holes.

2

3 Cutting out the shape

◆ Clamp the wood to your worktable with one of the marked sides overhanging the edge. With a saber saw, cut into the piece and follow the cutting line *(left)*. If a curve is too tight to cut without jamming the blade, back the saw out and cut from the opposite direction or veer off to the edge of the wood and start again.

◆ Once you've cut one side, stop the saw and turn the piece around, then cut the opposite side. Reposition the piece again to cut the two curved ends.

Adult's Corner...

4 Cutting the largest hole

It takes some strength to cut through a hardwood such as maple with a hole saw. If you notice the bit burning the wood, stop and let the bit cool before continuing.

♦ Clamp the spaghetti measure to the worktable on top of a piece of scrap wood.

♦ Fit your drill with a 1¾-inch hole saw. Set the bit at the marked center of the hole, then drill the hole through the measure *(left)*.

Drilling the other holes

To drill the remaining three spaghetti holes, use three spade bits sized 1½ inches, 1⅜ inches, and ⅞ inch.

♦ For each hole, set the center of the spade bit on the marked center point. Drill each hole through the wood and into the scrap piece *(right)*.

♦ For the hanger hole, fit the drill with a ¼-inch bit and drill at the marked center point. Cut the leather strip about 10 inches long, slip it through the hanger hole, and knot the ends together.

♦ Sand the surface of the measure and coat it with a nontoxic mineral- or vegetable-oil finish.

Building a Picture Frame

No picture is quite complete without a frame. And this traditional wooden frame, with two kinds of decorative molding, is the perfect companion for your favorite photo or work of art. It also makes a great, creative gift.

The 1x3 pine used in this project is a good size for framing an 8x10 picture. The cove molding on the inside edges helps hold the picture in place and gives the frame a more decorative look. Corner molding on the outside finishes the edges, hides the fasteners, and adds a nice finishing touch.

Materials you'll need

Wood	5 feet 1x3 pine 5 feet 1x1 molding 4 feet ½-inch cove molding
Hardware	Small screw eyes and picture wire Picture pivots
Fasteners	#6 1½-inch screws ¾-inch finishing nails 1-inch finishing nails
Miscellaneous	Wood glue 8x10 cardboard backing 8x10 picture-frame glass

The tools you'll need...

Tape measure

Screwdrivers

Putty knife

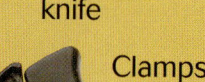
Utility knife

Clamps

Awl

Hammer

How the pieces fit together...

- The 1x3 framing is held together by screws driven through the corners.

- Cove molding cut to fit the inside of the framing is glued and nailed in place.

- Corner molding is cut to fit around the framing and attached with nails.

- Pivots hold the picture, cardboard, and glass in place.

- The frame is hung with small screw eyes and picture wire.

Corner molding: sides (2)
13⅝" x 1" x 1"

Corner molding: top and bottom (2)
15½" x 1" x 1"

Cardboard
10" x 8"

Pivots (4)

Glass
10" x 8"

Framing: sides (2)
13" x 2½" x ¾"

Cove molding: sides (2)
8⅛" x ½" x ½"

Cove molding: top and bottom (2)
10" x ½" x ½"

Framing: top and bottom (2)
15" x 2½" x ¾"

Did You Know...

How to Choose Picture-Frame Glass and Mats

If you'll be framing a watercolor painting or a photograph, protect and enhance it with a covering of glass. Nonglare glass is great for bright rooms, where sunlight can cause reflections. But for pictures that have a lot of detail, standard clear glass is the better choice.

If the picture you want to frame is a little too small, the space between it and the frame can be filled with a mat. Mats are made from a thick colored card that fits like a window around the picture. You'll find there's a wide variety of mat colors available. Choose one that doesn't draw too much attention away from the picture and fits well with the color of your frame and the painting or photograph it surrounds.

Backsaw

Wire cutters

Miter box

Nail set

Electric drill with #6 combination bit

Straightedge

Preparing the framing

Before measuring the framing for your first cut, cut one end at a 45-degree angle.

♦ Lay a 1x3 flat in a miter box. With a backsaw, make a 45-degree cut near one end *(right)*. Label the cut end A.

The Miter Box

The best way to cut angled corners by hand is with a miter box. Some fancy models come with their own saw attached and can be adjusted to make cuts at any angle from 0 to 90 degrees. The one featured in this project is a simple three-sided box with slots in the sides for making cuts at 45 and 90 degrees. Use a backsaw with a miter box. Its rigid blade will cut straighter than the more flexible blade of a crosscut saw.

Cutting the framing

♦ Lay a ruler or tape measure along what will be the inside edge of the top frame piece. Measure and mark a point 10 inches from the end of the first cut *(left)*.

♦ Saw the frame piece at the mark, cutting it in the miter box at a 45-degree angle opposite the first. Label the cut end B.

♦ Cut the remaining three pieces of the frame the same way, working your way around it. Remember to cut the bottom piece 10 inches long and both sides 8⅛ inches long. Label the cut ends C through H as you go.

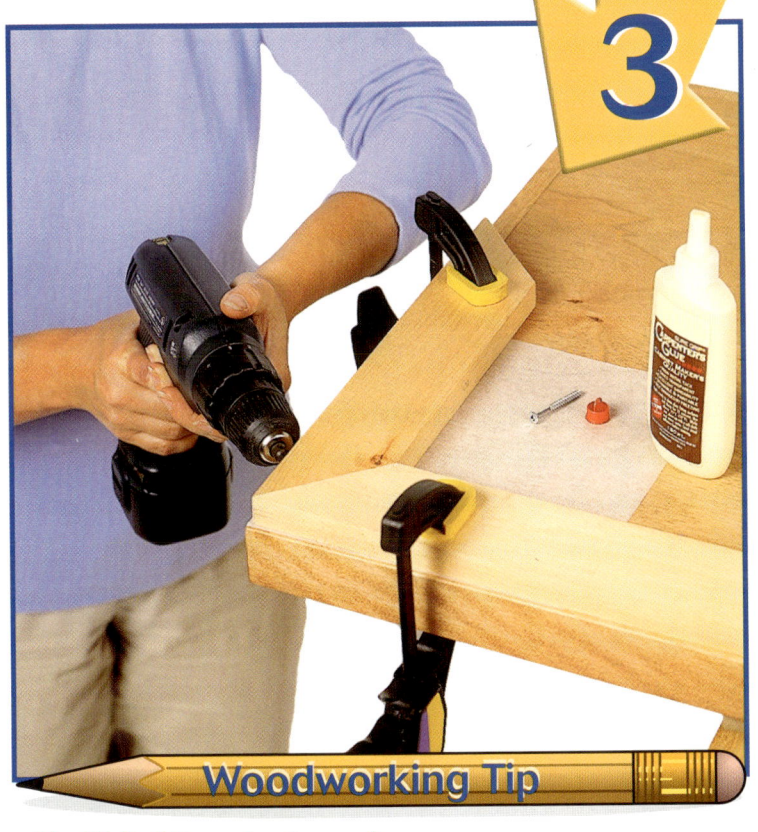

3

Assembling the frame

♦ Run a bead of wood glue along the end of the top frame piece labeled B and along the end of the side piece labeled C. Clamp the pieces face up on your worktable with the glued ends pressed together.

♦ Mark a point on the outside edge of one piece 1¾ inches from the corner. Mark the other piece the same way, measuring from the same corner. Join the two points with a pencil line across the top of the pieces.

♦ Fit a combination bit in your drill and adjust the bit for a ³⁄₈-inch-deep counterbore hole. Drill a hole into the edge of a frame piece at one of the marked points, aligning the bit with the pencil line *(left)*. Center the hole between the faces of the frame piece.

♦ Drive a wood screw into the hole so the head sits at the bottom of the counterbore portion. Assemble the rest of the frame this way.

Woodworking Tip

You'll find it easier to work on the corners of the frame if you clamp the two pieces directly above the corner of your table.

Preparing the cove molding

♦ Lay the molding in the miter box with the thicker side against the near side of the box. With the backsaw, make a 45-degree cut near one end *(right)*.

4

5

Cutting the cove molding

♦ Lay the frame face down on the table and align the cut end of the molding with the inside of the corner labeled A and H. Make a mark on the molding in line with corner B and C *(left)*.

♦ Saw the molding at the mark, cutting it in the miter box at a 45-degree angle opposite the first. Label the molding A-B to remind you to match it with the frame piece at the top of the frame.

♦ Work your way around the frame, cutting and labeling the other molding pieces in the same way.

6

Fastening the cove molding

♦ Measure and mark two points on the inside face of each piece of molding 2 inches from each end.

♦ At each mark, tap a 3/4-inch finishing nail partway into the molding.

♦ On one of the molding pieces, run a bead of glue along the face that will sit on the framing. Stand the frame on the side the molding goes with, position the molding on the frame, and drive the two nails into the framing *(right)*. Glue and nail the remaining pieces of cove molding in place.

Preparing the corner molding

Aligning a straightedge with the corner of the frame and extending the joint to the corner molding with a pencil will give you a straight line to follow when cutting the molding.

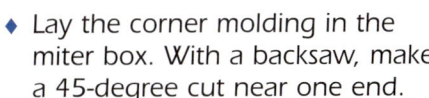

- ◆ Lay the corner molding in the miter box. With a backsaw, make a 45-degree cut near one end.

- ◆ Lay the frame face down on the table and align the cut end of the molding with the outside of the corner labeled A and H. Turn the frame over. With a straightedge, make a mark on the molding in line with corner B and C *(left)*.

Cutting the molding

- ◆ Saw the molding at the mark, cutting it in the miter box at a 45-degree angle opposite the first *(right)*. Label the molding so you know where it goes on the frame.

- ◆ Work your way around the frame, cutting and labeling the other molding pieces in the same way.

Fastening the molding

◆ Measure and mark two points on the outside edge of each piece of molding 2 inches from each end. At each mark, tap a 1-inch finishing nail partway into the molding.

◆ Stand the frame on the side opposite to the one the molding goes with and position the molding on the frame, making sure the outside face of the molding is flush with the back of the frame. Drive the two nails into the framing *(right)*.

◆ Nail the remaining pieces of corner molding in place, applying a bead of glue on both ends of each piece before positioning it.

◆ With a nail set and the hammer, sink all the nail heads in the corner and cove molding.

◆ With a putty knife, fill the nail holes with wood filler. Let the filler dry, then sand the surface of the frame with 120-grit sandpaper.

Adding the picture pivots and wire

◆ With a utility knife, cut a piece of cardboard backing the same size as your picture and glass.

◆ Set the frame face down and fasten a picture pivot to each frame piece near the inside edge and centered between the ends.

◆ Screw small screw eyes into the side pieces an inch or so above the middle. Then, with wire cutters, snip a length of picture wire a little longer than the distance between the eyes *(left)* and attach the ends to the eyes.

◆ Paint the frame to match your picture.

◆ Lay the glass, picture, and cardboard backing in the frame, then swivel the pivots against the backing to secure it in place.

Chapter 4
Projects for the Home

Building a CD Rack

"Keep it simple"—good advice for anyone just learning woodworking. This little desktop CD rack is so easy to build that even the youngest of beginners can help put it together.

If you've got a 2-foot piece of 1x6 hanging around, you've got enough wood for a CD rack. With a 4-foot length, make two and give one away as a gift. The rack featured here, with its 12-inch base, holds up to 27 CDs. Protect the wood with some stain or have fun painting the rack in wild colors.

Materials you'll need

Wood	2 feet 1x6 pine
Fasteners	1 1/2-inch finishing nails
Miscellaneous	Wood glue
	Wood filler

The tools you'll need...

Putty knife

Try square

Tape measure

Nail set

Hammer

Clamps

Sanding block and 120-grit sandpaper

Electric drill with 1/32-inch twist bit

How the pieces fit together...

♦ The upright is nailed to the top of the base flush with one end. The support piece is attached to the underside of the base at the other end.

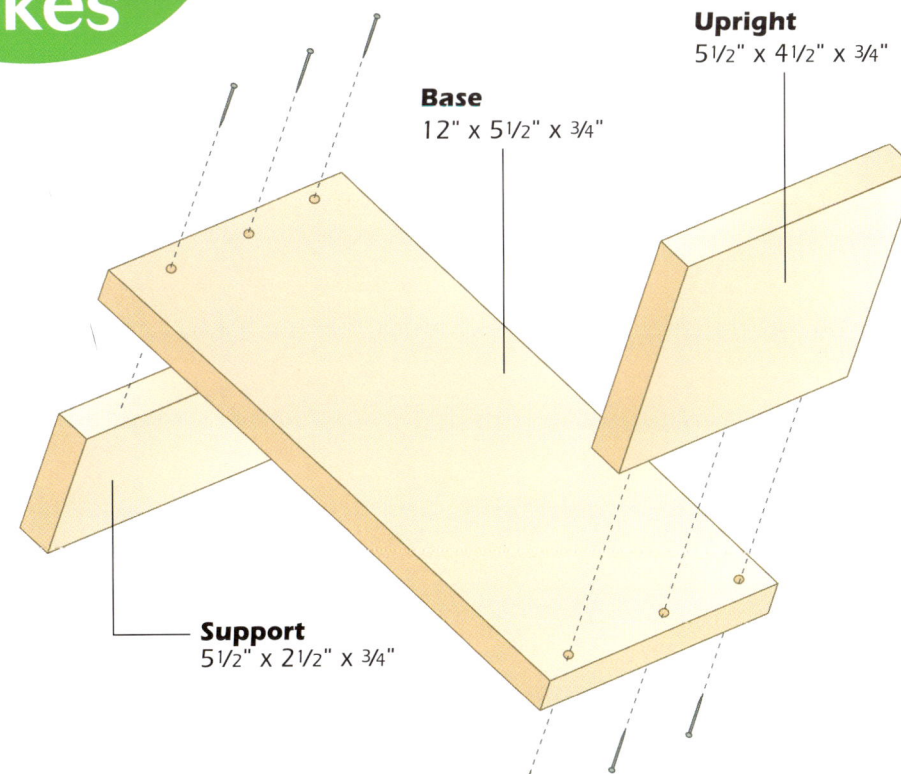

Upright
5½" x 4½" x ¾"

Base
12" x 5½" x ¾"

Support
5½" x 2½" x ¾"

Did You Know...

Setting the Record Straight

Before there were CDs and CD players, most recorded music came to us on flat, black plastic disks called "records," short for recordings. In 1887 German inventor Emile Berliner created a flat disk made of hard rubber to play recorded music on another of his inventions, the gramophone (right). Soon Berliner's records were being mass-produced and sold to a public hungry for music. Played at a speed of 78 revolutions per minute (RPM), the first records were turned by cranking the gramophone by hand. Many improvements to both records and record players were made in the years that followed. By 1948 sturdier records were being made from a type of plastic called "vinyl." Long-playing 10-inch records, called "LPs" or "albums," were now recorded and played by mechanized record players at 33 ⅓ RPM. Seven-inch "singles" were played at 45 RPM. Not much changed in the way we bought and listened to music until the early 1980s, when the Sony and Philips companies introduced the compact disk, or CD, we know today. The first music CD is thought to be Billy Joel's 52nd Street, released in 1982. In 1988, for the first time, more CDs were sold than vinyl records, and by the early 1990s all of the major record companies had virtually stopped making vinyl records altogether.

Marking nailing lines

The nails that fasten the base to the upright and support will be driven along the nailing lines marked here.

♦ Cut the pieces of the CD rack to length.

♦ Mark a point along each edge of the base 3/8 inch from one end. With a try square, connect the marks with a line across the face *(left)*.

♦ Turn over the base and mark a line at the other end the same way.

Drilling nail holes

Nails can split wood, especially when you drive them near the end of a board. Drill pilot holes first to prevent splitting.

♦ To protect your worktable, clamp the base down on top of a piece of scrap wood.

♦ Fit your electric drill with a 1/32-inch bit. Drill a hole along the nailing line about 1/2 inch from each edge of the base and two more holes spaced equally in between *(right)*. Turn over the base and drill pilot holes in the same locations on the other side.

Woodworking Tip

Instead of nailing straight into a board, try driving the nails at a slight angle. This will help make the joint between the two pieces even stronger. When you're drilling pilot holes first, drill them at an angle, too.

3 ## Assembling the rack

- Clamp the upright face up to the table.

- Drive a nail partway into each pilot hole at one end of the base, then run a bead of wood glue across the opposite face of the base in line with the nails. Position the base against the upright with the edges of both pieces aligned and drive the nails all the way *(left)*.

- Clamp the support to the table and attach it to the other side of the base the same way.

Finishing touches

- With a nail set and the hammer, sink the nail heads below the surface of the wood.

- With a putty knife, cover the nail holes with wood filler *(right)*.

- Sand the surface of the rack with 120-grit sandpaper in a sanding block. Smooth any sharp edges. Then, feel free to decorate your rack any way you want. The one featured here was painted black and decorated with strips of colored tape to simulate the look of a piano keyboard. You can also apply a clear finish or paint the rack another color.

4

Personalizing Your CD Rack

You can adapt the size of the rack to suit your CD collection. The clear-finish version *(upper near right)*, with its 18-inch base, can hold up to 42 CDs. The yellow-painted rack *(lower right)* has a 24-inch rack for up to 57 discs. As you lengthen the base, cut the support taller by the same proportion. The support on the clear rack is 3¾ inches tall, one-and-one-half times taller than the original. The yellow rack support is 5 inches tall, double the original.

Building a Bookcase

Hitting the books might be more fun when you've helped build your own bookcase. The shelves in this one are adjustable, so you'll be able to organize your books according to height. For example, you can space the shelves so as to put tall books on one shelf and short books on another.

This project may be a bit more challenging than the others in this book. Although the techniques aren't difficult, the pieces of the bookcase are bulky and awkward to handle. To get started on the right foot, have the pieces cut to size at the lumberyard.

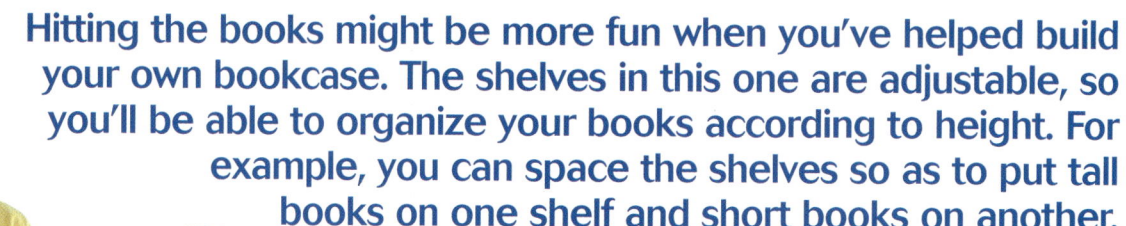

Materials you'll need

Wood	34 inches x 24 inches 1/4-inch hardboard, MDF, or plywood
	48 inches x 48 inches 3/4-inch veneered plywood (birch, cherry, oak, or maple)
	20 feet 7/8-inch pre-glued edge banding
Hardware	3 13/4-inch x 1-inch angle brackets
	8 shelf pins
	4 plastic leg tips
Fasteners	#6 11/2-inch screws
	#6 5/8-inch screws
	1-inch common nails
Miscellaneous	Wood glue
	Wood filler

The tools you'll need...

Tape measure

Screwdrivers

File

Scissors

Straightedge

Roller

Sanding block and 120-grit sandpaper

The time it takes

3 hours to build
1 hour to finish

How the pieces fit together...

♦ The top and bottom are attached between the sides with screws. Wood plugs cover the screw heads.

♦ Two adjustable shelves sit on shelf pins that fit in holes drilled in the sides.

♦ The kick plate fits between the sides and is fastened to the underside of the bottom.

♦ The back is nailed to the top, bottom, and sides.

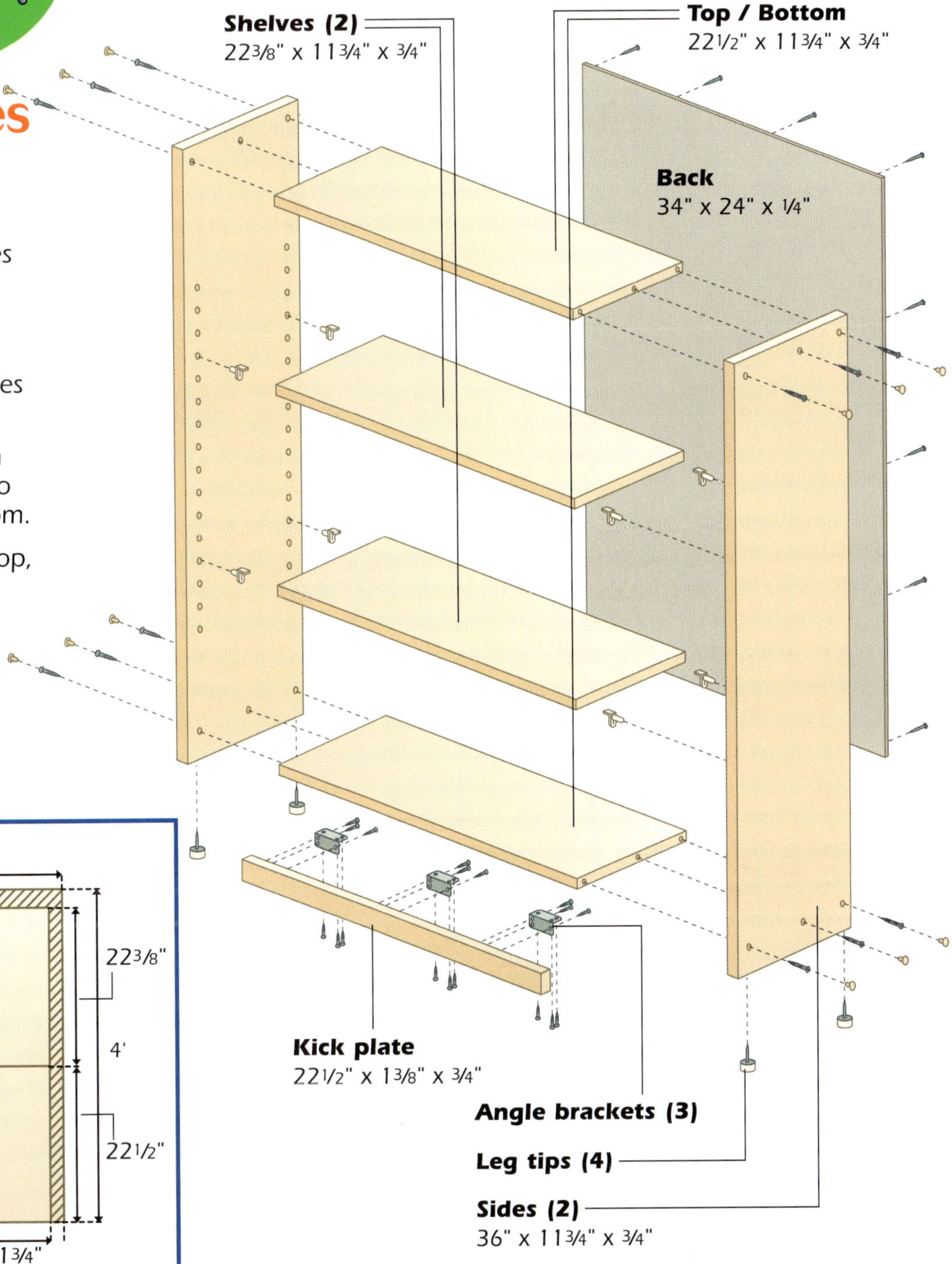

Shelves (2)
22³⁄₈" x 11³⁄₄" x ³⁄₄"

Top / Bottom
22¹⁄₂" x 11³⁄₄" x ³⁄₄"

Back
34" x 24" x ¹⁄₄"

Kick plate
22¹⁄₂" x 1³⁄₈" x ³⁄₄"

Angle brackets (3)

Leg tips (4)

Sides (2)
36" x 11³⁄₄" x ³⁄₄"

Cutting Pattern

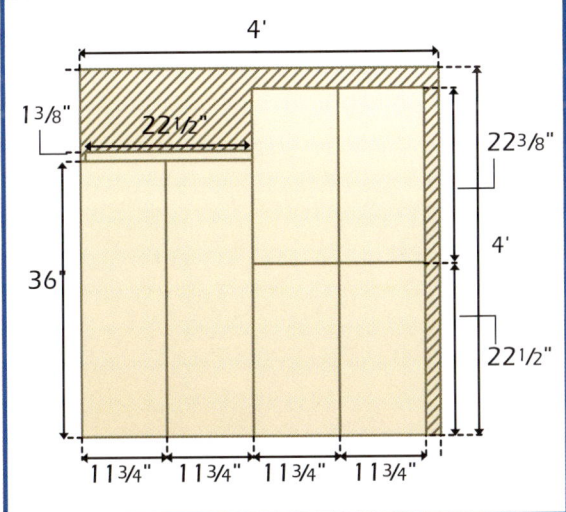

4'

1³⁄₈"

22¹⁄₂"

22³⁄₈"

4'

36"

22¹⁄₂"

11³⁄₄" 11³⁄₄" 11³⁄₄" 11³⁄₄"

Clamps

Hammer

Iron

Electric drill with 3/16- and 3/32-inch twist bits and #6 combination bit

Preparing the edge banding

The bookcase shown here is made from veneered plywood, a type of plywood covered with thin sheets of hardwood. It looks like solid wood, but costs less. Any cut edges that will be visible when the project is assembled need to be covered with a wood product called edge banding to hide the exposed plywood. These include the front edges and top ends of the sides, and the front edges of the top, bottom, and shelves. You can get banding that matches the veneer covering the plywood.

♦ Hold a corner of one of the pieces in a clamp, then secure the clamp to your worktable so the edge that needs banding is facing up.

♦ With a helper, unroll enough banding to cover the edge. Using scissors, cut a strip that overlaps the edge by about 1 inch *(left)*.

Bonding the edge banding

Most edge banding has heat-activated glue on the bottom. A clothing iron is the best tool for softening the glue so it will adhere to the wood under it. A bit of glue may stick to the iron, so use an old one, if possible, or place a cloth or paper between the iron and the banding. It's a good idea to cut a short strip of banding and practice sticking it on a piece of scrap wood to get a feel for the technique.

♦ Set the iron to "Cotton" or "High" and let it heat up. With a helper, reposition the cut strip of banding on the wood edge. Holding the strip down near one end, begin passing the iron over it toward the other end *(right)*. Keep the iron moving at all times. If not, you risk burning the edge banding.

♦ Use your free hand to flatten the banding ahead of the iron as you work. Move the iron back and forth along the edge until the banding is firmly attached to the wood. Run a hand roller over the edge to help the banding adhere.

Adult's Corner...

Trimming the edge banding

There are different ways to trim edge banding flush: You can use a utility knife and sanding block or a special trimming tool. Instead of investing in this tool, try a laminate file. A regular wood file works, too, if you use it carefully.

♦ Cut the overlapping edge banding at both ends of the piece with scissors.

♦ Holding the file at an angle, gently push it forward along one side of the edge *(right)*. Work in the direction of the wood grain of the banding, not against it. The excess banding should begin to peel off. File along the edge until the banding is flush with the side. Also file away any excess glue. File the other side of the edge the same way.

♦ Fit a sanding block with 120-grit sandpaper and sand the edges and ends of the piece smooth. Repeat steps 1 through 3 to attach edge banding to the remaining edges that will be exposed.

3

Trimming excess edge banding can be difficult. If you're not careful, the banding can tear or break, exposing the plywood below and ruining the work you just did. Work carefully—if at all possible, practice on a scrap piece before trying the real thing.

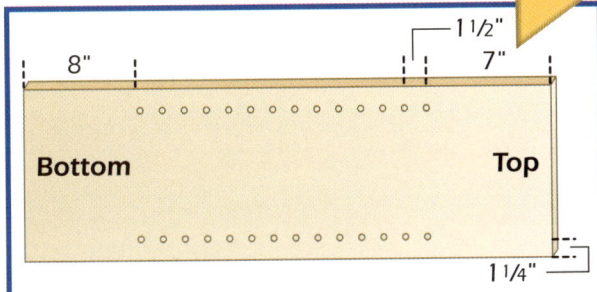

4

Marking the shelf holes

Each adjustable shelf sits on four shelf pins that fit in holes drilled into the inside faces of the sides. A pair of holes in each side every 1 1/2 inches let the shelves sit at different heights. For the shelves to be level, each pair of holes must be level with each other and with those on the opposite side. Refer to the inset diagram to help you mark the holes.

♦ Set one side inside face up on the worktable. Measure and mark two lines along the face 1 1/4 inches from each edge.

♦ Starting 7 inches from the top and 8 inches from the bottom, mark a shelf hole along each line every 1/2 inches *(left)*. Mark shelf holes on the other side piece.

1 1/2"

8"   7"

Bottom   Top

1 1/4"

Drilling shelf holes

The shelf holes should be only as deep as the length of the shafts of the shelf pins. Those used here are 3/8 inch long.

5

◆ Fit an electric drill with a 3/16-inch bit. Wrap a strip of masking tape around the bit 3/8 inch from the tip. You can also use a stop collar to mark the drilling depth.

◆ Holding the drill as straight as possible, drill a hole into the side at each mark *(right)*. Stop drilling when the masking tape or stop collar contacts the surface.

Woodworking Tip

A hole-drilling jig is a quick and easy alternative to marking holes by hand, especially if you'll be making more than one bookcase. It's more precise, too.

Mark your shelf holes on a 2- or 3-inch-wide strip of 1/4-inch particleboard or plywood as long as the bookcase sides (upper far left). Drill a hole through the jig at each mark (upper near left). To use the jig, clamp it on top of a side piece, making sure its edges and ends are flush with those of the side. Using the holes in the jig as a guide, drill holes into the side piece as you did in step 5 (lower left). The only wrinkle is that you'll have to account for the thickness of the jig when marking the drilling depth on the bit.

6 Marking the assembly holes

The bookcase is held together with screws driven through the sides into the top and bottom.

♦ Set one side face down on the table. Measure and mark two lines across the piece, one 7/8 inch from the top and the other 1 7/8 from the bottom *(inset)*.

♦ On each line, measure and mark screw holes 1 1/2 inches from each edge *(left)*. Make a third mark at the midpoint of each line, then mark identical screw holes on the other side piece.

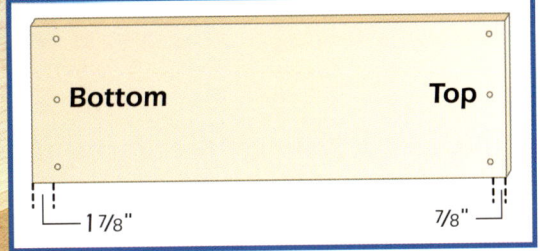

Bottom   Top

├ 1 7/8" ┤   ├ 7/8" ┤

Drilling the assembly holes

To hide the screw heads with wood plugs, you'll need to drill counterbore holes.

♦ Clamp a side piece face down to the table, placing a piece of scrap wood under the marked holes. Fit a combination bit in the drill and adjust the bit for a 1/2-inch counter-bore hole.

♦ Holding the drill as straight as possible, drill a hole into the side at each marked screw hole *(right)*. Drill the holes at the opposite end and at both ends of the other side piece.

♦ Unless you intend to paint the bookcase, erase or sand off the pencil lines on both side pieces.

7

Clamping the case

A couple of long clamps (about 24 inches) will come in handy when assembling a project as wide as this bookcase. If your clamps aren't long enough, have helpers hold the pieces steady during assembly.

♦ Cut two spacers to maintain the gap between the top and bottom and the ends of the sides. Make both spacers 11¾ inches long, with the bottom one 1½ inches wide and the top one ½ inch wide.

♦ With a helper, set the two sides on edge on the table with their shelf holes facing each other and the edge banding facing down.

♦ Place the bottom between the sides with one edge of the 1½-inch-width spacer against the bottom and the other edge flush with the end of one side. Tighten two clamps on the sides in line with the bottom to hold the assembly (above). Be sure the clamps don't cover the holes in the sides.

Drilling pilot holes in the bottom

Drill pilot holes into the bottom to prevent the screws you will use to attach it to the sides from splitting the wood.

♦ Fit the drill with a ³/32-inch bit and drill pilot holes in the bottom, using the holes in the sides as a guide (left).

10

Attaching the bottom

♦ Attach the sides to the bottom by driving a 1 1/2-inch screw into each hole *(left)*.

♦ Repeat steps 8 through 10 to fasten the top to the sides, using the 1/2-inch-width spacer to help position it.

Attaching the back

♦ Set the back face up on the table, then measure and mark lines around its perimeter 3/8 inch from the edges and ends.

♦ Lay the bookcase face down on the table, then place the back on top with its marked lines facing up.

♦ Making sure the back is flush with the top, bottom, and sides of the case, nail it in place along the marked lines. Drive a nail at each corner, every 4 inches along the top and bottom, and every 8 1/2 inches or so along the sides *(right)*.

12 Attaching the brackets to the kick plate

The kick plate is usually set in from the sides and bottom by about 3/8 inch to leave room for your toes when standing at the bookcase.

♦ Mark two points on the kick plate 2 inches from each end and a third point midway between the ends. Center an angle bracket on each point so the upright flange is flush with the top edge of the plate, then mark its screw holes on the plate.

♦ Fit an electric drill with a 3/32-inch bit and wrap a strip of masking tape around it 1/2 inch from the tip. Drill a hole into the kick plate at each mark, stopping when the tape contacts the wood.

♦ Attach the brackets to the plate with 5/8-inch screws (left).

Attaching the kick plate

♦ Cut a 3/8-inch-thick board to fit between the sides as a spacer for the kick plate. With the bookcase face down on the table, place the spacer between the sides and against the bottom.

♦ Set the kick plate on the spacer so the bracket flanges are flat against the bottom. Mark the bracket screw holes on the bottom.

♦ Set the kick plate and spacer aside, then drill a hole into the bottom at each mark as you did in step 12.

♦ Reposition the kick plate and fasten it to the bottom of the bookcase (right).

13

Adding wood plugs

Use decorative wood plugs to hide the heads of the screws in the sides.

♦ Dab wood glue on the ends of the wood plugs and push them into the screw holes on the sides of the bookcase *(right)*.

♦ Gently tap the plugs with a hammer, if necessary, to seat them in the holes.

14

15

Attaching leg tips

Attach plastic leg tips to the bottom of the sides at the front and back to keep the bookcase slightly off the ground.

♦ With the case still face down, measure 1/2 inch from each corner and make a mark on the bottom of the side pieces.

♦ Set a leg tip on each mark and tack it in place with a hammer *(left)*.

♦ Fit a pair of shelf pins in each side for each shelf and install the shelves.

Building a Pet Bed

Is your dog hogging the bed? Is your couch covered in cat hair? If so, your pet needs a bed of its own. We'll show you here how to make one. All you have to do is provide the cozy cushion.

The bed we made is large enough to accommodate an average-size dog, but you can adjust the measurements to make the box as big or small as you like. For a cat bed, you might want to knock 6 or 8 inches off the length of each piece. Once the bed is built, put it somewhere special, such as in a quiet nook or a sunny corner.

Materials you'll need

Wood	8 feet 1x6 pine
	24 inches x 18½ inches
	¾-inch plywood
Fasteners	1½-inch finishing nails
Miscellaneous	Wood glue
	Wood filler

The tools you'll need...

Tape measure

Nail set

Putty knife

Straightedge

Sanding block and 120-grit sandpaper

How the pieces fit together...

- The sides are glued and nailed to the ends of the bottom.

- The front and back are glued and nailed to the edges of the bottom and the ends of the sides.

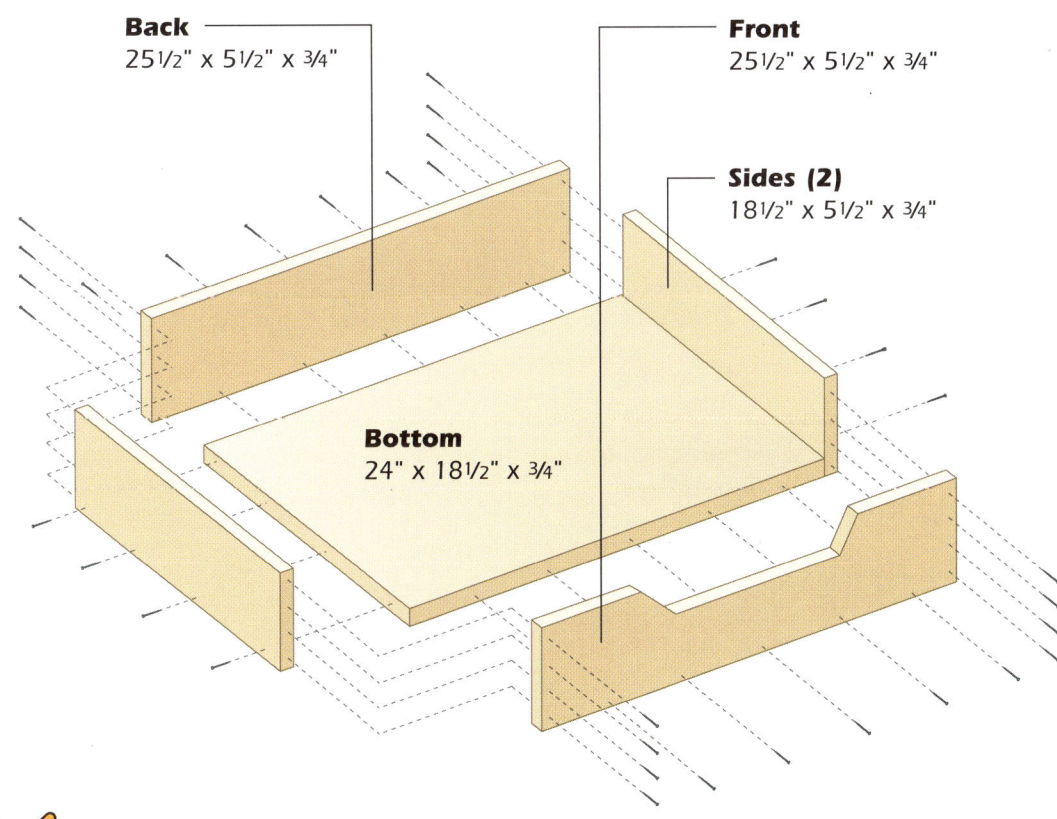

Back
25½" x 5½" x ¾"

Front
25½" x 5½" x ¾"

Sides (2)
18½" x 5½" x ¾"

Bottom
24" x 18½" x ¾"

Did You Know...

Population Explosion

Over 70,000 puppies and kittens are born in the U.S. every day. There are currently about 70 million cats and 60 million dogs in the U.S. Luckily most of them lead comfortable lives with responsible owners. Some even have their own beds. However, overpopulation is a serious problem. Sadly, nearly 10 million animals are put to sleep every year because there is nobody to care for them. Do your part to help control the pet population. Unless you have a very good reason not to, talk to your veterinarian about having your pet spayed or neutered.

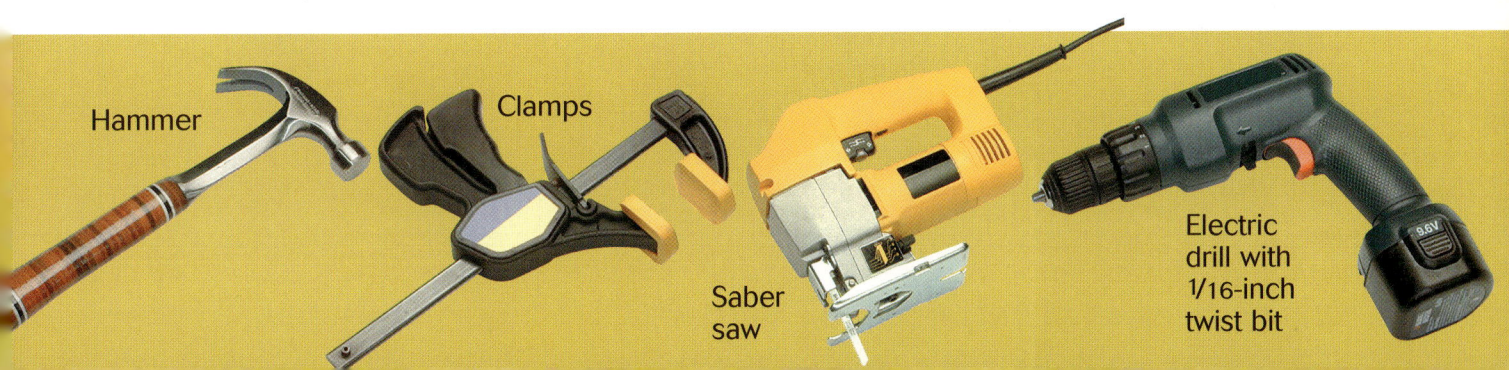

Hammer

Clamps

Saber saw

Electric drill with 1/16-inch twist bit

5"   5"

2"   2"

2"   2"

25 1/2"

Marking the opening in the front

The front of the bed features an opening that allows your pet to easily climb in and out.

♦ Cut the pieces of the pet bed to size.

♦ Measure and mark two points on the top edge of the front 5 inches from each end. Measure straight down 2 inches from each point and mark a small X. Using a try square, connect each point to the X below it with a vertical line, then use a ruler or a straightedge to join the Xs with a horizontal line.

♦ Mark a point 2 inches from each end of the horizontal line, then connect each point to the point on the top edge with a diagonal line *(left)*. The diagonal and horizontal lines represent the opening in the front *(inset)*.

Adult's Corner...

Cutting the opening

The cutting line for the opening angles too sharply for a saber saw blade to make the cut in a single pass. You'll have to make three separate cuts to create the opening. Avoid cutting beyond the marked lines—or you'll have to start over with a new piece. Work slowly and carefully.

♦ Clamp the front to your worktable with the marked opening overhanging it. Align the blade of a saber saw with the end of one diagonal line. Start the saw and slowly feed the blade into the piece. Cut along the line until you reach the horizontal line *(upper right)*. Cut the other diagonal line the same way.

♦ Feed the blade into the piece about 3 inches from the first cut. Cut a gentle curve until you meet the horizontal line, then cut straight along it to the end of the second diagonal cut *(center right)*.

♦ Remove the remaining piece of waste wood from the opening by cutting along the horizontal line until you reach the end of the first diagonal cut *(lower right)*.

Drilling pilot holes

To prevent splitting of the wood as you nail the bed together, drill pilot holes into the front, back, and side pieces.

♦ On all four pieces, mark a horizontal line along the front face 3/8 inch from the bottom edge. On the front and back, mark vertical lines across the face 3/8 inch from the edges.

♦ Clamp the front to the table on top of a piece of scrap wood. Fit an electric drill with a 1/16-inch bit, then drill a hole through the front at each bottom corner where the lines cross. Also drill holes every 4 or 5 inches along the horizontal line *(left)* and every 1 1/2 inches along the vertical lines. Drill holes through the back the same way and along the horizontal lines on the sides.

Attaching the sides

♦ Clamp the bottom face up to the table. Drive a nail partway into each pilot hole in one side, then run a bead of wood glue across the opposite face of the side in line with the nails.

♦ With a helper, position the side against the bottom with the edges of both pieces aligned and drive the nails all the way *(right)*.

♦ Undo the clamp and reposition the assembly on the table, then attach the second side piece to the bottom the same way.

Attaching the back

♦ Clamp the assembly down so the back edge of the bottom is even with an edge of the table.

♦ Run a thin bead of wood glue along the back end of the sides and bottom.

♦ Position the back against the sides and bottom so the pieces align *(left)*.

♦ Nail the back to the sides and bottom.

Attaching the front

♦ Reposition the bed on the table so the front edge of the bottom is even with the table's edge.

♦ Attach the front to the sides and bottom as you did the back with glue and nails *(right)*.

7

Covering the nail heads

♦ With a helper holding the bed steady, use a nail set and a hammer to sink all of the nail heads below the surface.

♦ Cover the nail holes with wood filler using a putty knife. Smooth the filler with the knife *(left)* and let it dry.

8

Sanding the bed

♦ Fit a sanding block with 120-grit sandpaper and smooth out any rough spots or sharp edges on the bed. Hold the block at an angle as you work to round all of the edges.

♦ Pay special attention to the opening at the front of the bed. Its edges will be jagged from the saber saw blade. Put a little extra muscle into the sanding block, angling it to sand a slight bevel or angle in the edges *(right)*.

Building a Table & Bench

This small table and bench set is just the right size for the little tyke who loves to draw, do puzzles, or make a big old mess with paper and glue or even clay. Sound like anyone you might know?

They may look complicated once they are built, but the table and bench are actually simple to put together. There are no fancy joints here, just screws, nails, and some nuts and bolts. Depending on your needs, you can make both or just one, or you can double the fun and make a second bench so the table can be shared with a little friend.

Materials you'll need

TABLE

Wood	24 inches x 18 inches 3/4-inch MDF 6 feet 2x2 pine 7 feet 1x2 pine
Hardware	8 2½-inch x ¼-inch carriage bolts 8 2½-inch x ¾-inch angle brackets
Fasteners	1½-inch finishing nails #6 ⅝-inch screws
Miscellaneous	Wood glue Wood filler

BENCH

Wood	3 feet 1x8 pine 12 inches 1x4 pine
Fasteners	#8 2-inch screws 1½-inch finishing nails
Miscellaneous	Wood glue Wood filler

The tools you'll need...

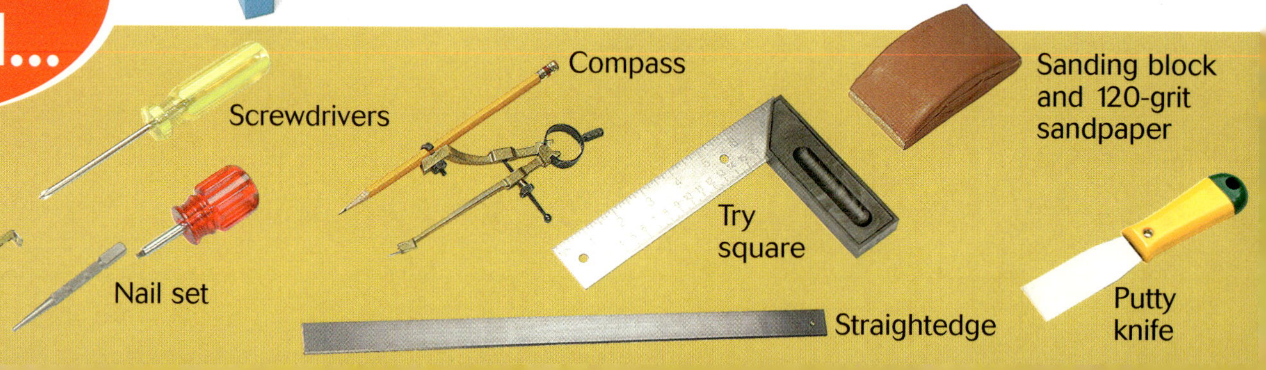

Tape measure

Screwdrivers

Nail set

Compass

Try square

Straightedge

Sanding block and 120-grit sandpaper

Putty knife

How the pieces fit together...

TABLE

♦ The skirt anchors the tabletop with angle brackets. The four pieces of the skirt are nailed together at the corners.

♦ The legs are bolted to the skirt at each corner.

BENCH

♦ The legs are screwed to the support.

♦ The seat is nailed to the legs and support.

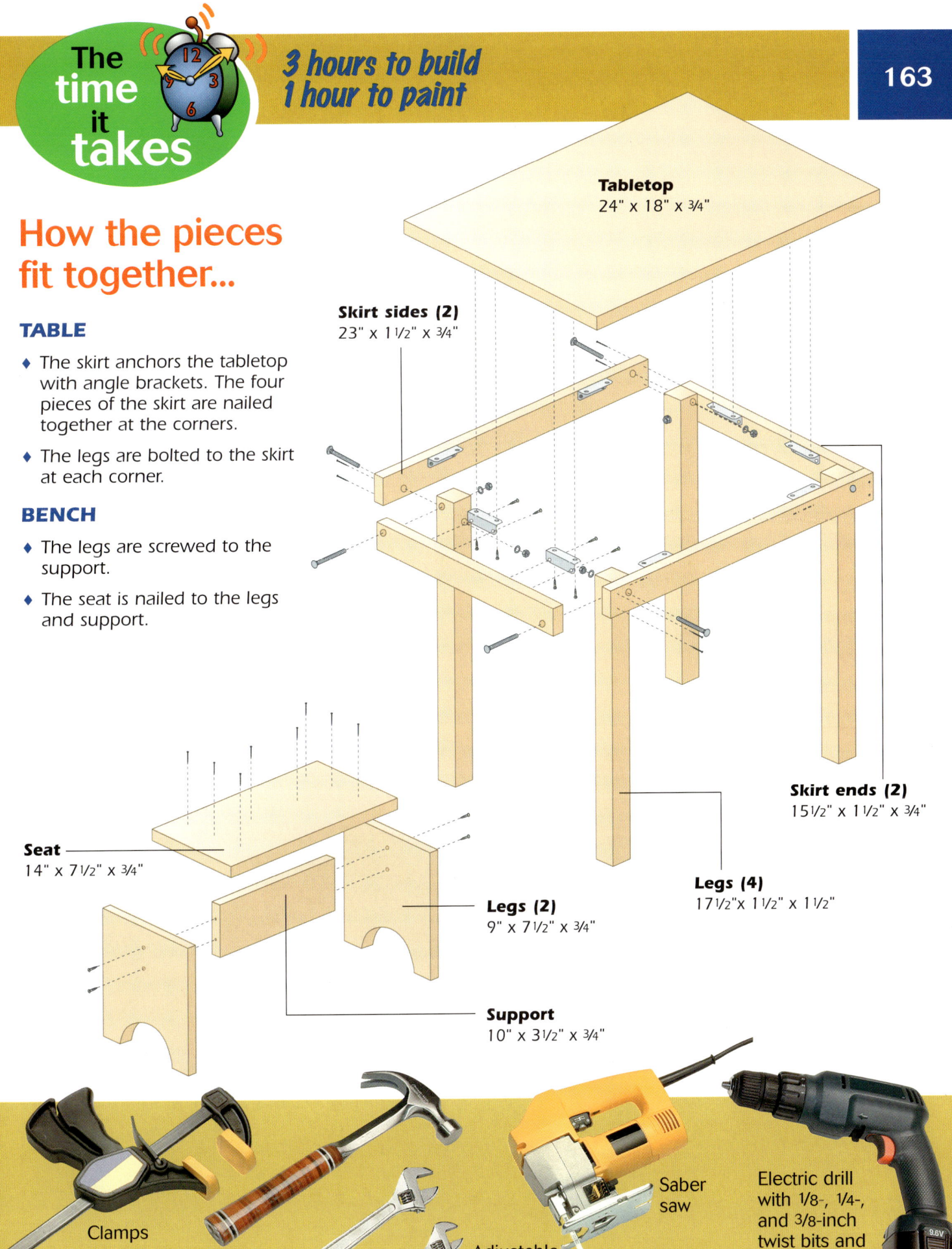

Tabletop
24" x 18" x 3/4"

Skirt sides (2)
23" x 1 1/2" x 3/4"

Skirt ends (2)
15 1/2" x 1 1/2" x 3/4"

Legs (4)
17 1/2" x 1 1/2" x 1 1/2"

Seat
14" x 7 1/2" x 3/4"

Legs (2)
9" x 7 1/2" x 3/4"

Support
10" x 3 1/2" x 3/4"

Clamps

Hammer

Adjustable wrenches

Saber saw

Electric drill with 1/8-, 1/4-, and 3/8-inch twist bits and #8 combination bit

Making the Table

Attaching the brackets

Attach the brackets to the sides and ends of the skirt before fastening them to the underside of the tabletop.

♦ Cut the pieces of the table to size.

♦ On the skirt boards, mark a point 3 inches from each end on the piece.

♦ Align the edge of a 2½-inch angle bracket with a marked point on one of the skirt sides. With the upright flange of the bracket flush with one edge of the side, attach the bracket in place with two ⅝-inch screws *(left)*. Attach a second bracket to the piece at the other marked point and at both marks on the other pieces of the skirt.

Marking a skirt side on the tabletop

♦ If one side of the top is more attractive than the other, set it good face down on the worktable.

♦ Measuring along one of the longer edges of the top, mark a line 4¼ inches from one end.

♦ Extend the line a few inches across the top with a try square *(right)*.

3 Attaching the skirt side

- Cut a ½-inch-thick board about 6 inches long to fit as a spacer between the skirt and the edge of the tabletop.

- Set one of the skirt sides on the top so the outside edge of the bracket aligns with the marked line and its flanges are flat against the top.

- Hold the spacer against the skirt side and position the pieces so the outside face of the spacer is flush with the edge of the top. With a screwdriver, fasten the bracket to the top *(left)*.

- Fasten the bracket at the other end of the skirt side to the top, using the spacer to position the piece.

4 Attaching the opposite skirt side

- Position the two skirt ends on the top with one end of each piece against the skirt side you fastened in step 3, their outside faces flush with the ends of the skirt side. Position the second skirt side against the end pieces.

- With the ends of the second skirt side flush with the end pieces, clamp it in place and attach its brackets to the top *(right)*.

Fastening the ends of the skirt

In addition to being anchored to the top with brackets, the ends of the skirt are nailed to the sides to close the corners joining the pieces.

♦ Holding a skirt end steady, drive a nail through it and into the adjoining side piece *(left)*. Close the other corners of the skirt the same way.

♦ Fasten the brackets of both skirt ends to the tabletop.

5

Up Close...

Drilling the bolt holes

6

♦ Position one of the legs in a corner of the skirt. Clamp the leg to the skirt so its top end is flush against the tabletop.

♦ Fit a drill with a ¼-inch bit and drill a hole through the skirt and the leg about ½ inch from the top. Center the hole between the edges of the leg.

♦ Drill a second hole through the adjoining side of the skirt and leg, this time 1 inch from the top *(right)*. Drill bolt holes through the remaining legs at each of the remaining corners of the skirt.

The bolt holes need to be offset so the carriage bolts that fasten the legs to the skirt don't contact each other *(inset)*. Be careful to locate the holes at least ½ inch above the tabletop so that fitting washers and nuts over the bolts and tightening them with a wrench in step 7 won't be a problem.

Attaching the legs

7

- With one of the legs in position against the skirt and top, feed a carriage bolt through each hole in the skirt.

- Fit a washer and nut over each bolt, then tighten the bolts by hand. Tighten the bolts with an adjustable or open-end wrench *(right)*. Attach the remaining three legs the same way.

8

Finishing touches

All that's left to complete the table is hiding the nail heads and painting it any way you like.

- Use a nail set and a hammer to sink the nail heads at the corners of the skirt below the surface.

- With a putty knife, fill the nail holes with wood filler and spread it smooth *(left)*. Wait for the filler to dry, then sand it smooth with 120-grit sandpaper in a sanding block. Sand smooth any sharp edges on the table.

Making the Bench

Tracing the leg openings

The legs of the bench are 1x8 boards with a decorative arch cut out at one end.

♦ Cut the pieces of the bench to size.

♦ Place one of the legs flat on your worktable, then measure and mark the midpoint of the bottom end.

♦ Measure up 2 inches from the mark and make a second mark. Adjust the legs of a compass to span between the two marks, then trace the opening at the bottom of the leg *(right)*. Trace an identical opening on the other leg.

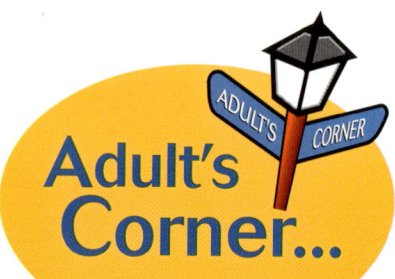

Adult's Corner...

Cutting the arcs in the legs

Cutting a tight arc like the one in the legs can be too much to handle for a youngster. The blade of the saber saw can bind and jam or break if it turns too tightly. The cut also needs to follow the line with precision so it looks smooth and not rough or jagged.

♦ Clamp a leg to the table so the the marked opening overhangs the edge.

♦ Cut along the line with a saber saw *(right)*. As you reach the end of the cut, use your free hand to hold the waste piece to keep it from tearing off the leg. Cut the opening in the other leg.

Marking the screws

Each leg is attached to the support with a pair of screws. Drill holes for them first to keep the fasteners from splitting the wood.

- Place one of the legs inside-face up on the table and mark the midpoint of the top end. Extend the point 3 to 4 inches with a try square *(left)*.

- Mark a screw hole along the line 1 inch and 2 1/2 inches from the top end.

Drilling screw holes

The screw holes need to be counter-sunk so the heads will be flush with the surface. If you want a more decorative look, drill counterbore holes and hide the screws with wood plugs *(see step 14, page 154)*.

- Fit an electric drill with a combination bit.

- Drill a countersink hole at each marked point *(right)*. Drill screw holes into the other leg the same way.

Drilling pilot holes

13

Drill pilot holes for the screws into the support to prevent the wood from splitting.

♦ Extend the line you marked on the legs in step 11 right to the bottom. Place the support on edge on the table, then mark a line along the edge that divides the width of the board in half (that'll be 3/8 inch from each face).

♦ Clamp a scrap board to the table and set the support against it with the marked line facing up. Hold a leg upside down against the support so the line on its inside face is even with the line on the support.

♦ Fit the drill with a 1/8-inch bit. Hold the leg steady and drill two pilot holes into the support, using the holes in the leg as guides *(right)*. Turn the support around and drill two pilot holes into its other end the same way.

Attaching the legs

14

♦ Spread a thin bead of wood glue along one end of the support. Press the support's other end against the scrap board, then reposition one of the legs against the glued end.

♦ Attach the leg to the support with screws *(below)*. Attach the leg to the other end of the support the same way.

Marking the seat

15

- With a ruler, measure and mark a horizontal line straight down the middle of the top.

- Mark a crossing vertical line between the edges of the top 2 inches from each end.

- Mark two points on the top where the lines cross and four more points, 1 1/2 inches from each end of the two vertical lines *(left)*. Mark two more points on the horizontal line 3 inches from each vertical line.

Attaching the seat

- Set the legs and support upright and center the top on them so the horizontal line on the top sits directly over the support and the vertical lines divide the legs in half.

- Drive a nail through the seat and into the legs and support at each marked point *(right)*.

16

17

Finishing the bench

- Sink all of the nail heads in the top below the surface with a hammer and nail set *(left)*.

- Fill all of the holes left by the nail heads with wood filler *(see step 8)* and let it dry. With a sanding block and 120-grit sandpaper, smooth over rough spots and sharp corners.

Glossary

A-B

Actual size: The real size of a board when it is sold. A 2x4, for example, is actually 1 1/2 inches thick and 3 1/2 inches wide.

Bow: A defect in wood in which a board laid flat curves up at the end.

C

Carriage bolt: A heavy-duty fastener that comes with a nut and a washer for joining pieces of wood together. A square shoulder just below the head of the bolt prevents it from turning and loosening after it is tightened.

Check: A defect in wood in which a board has cracks near the end.

Combination bit: A special drill bit fitted with a stop collar for drilling pilot holes, countersink holes, and counterbore holes for screws.

Counterbore hole: A hole that makes it possible to drive a screw below the wood surface so the head can be covered with a wood plug.

Countersink hole: A hole that makes it possible to drive a screw so the head ends up flush with the wood surface. The top part of the hole is wide enough to clear the screw head.

Cove molding: A type of decorative wood with a rounded profile.

Crook: A defect in wood in which a board laid on edge curves up at the end.

Crosscut: Sawing a board across the wood grain—usually across the width.

Cup: A defect in wood in which a board curves up at the edge.

D

Defect: A blemish in a piece of wood that reduces its strength or spoils its appearance.

Diameter: A line between any two points along the circumference or outside edge of a circle that also passes through its center; the diameter of a circle is twice as long as the radius.

Dowel: A cylindrical wood pin available in various diameters; dowels have many uses in woodworking, including shelf rails.

E

Edge: The narrow surface of a board. On a 2x4, for example (which is actually 1 1/2 inches by 3 1/2 inches), the edge is the 1 1/2-inch-wide surface.

Edge banding: Wood veneer that is glued to the cut edges of a piece of plywood or particleboard; available in rolls with heat-activated glue.

End grain: What you see when looking at the cut end of a board.

F

Face: The wide surface of a board. On a 2x4, for example (which is actually 1 1/2 inches by 3 1/2 inches), the face is the 3 1/2-inch-wide surface.

Frame: A rectangular assembly, usually with mitered corners, used to display pictures or artwork.

G

Grain: The direction and pattern of the wood fibers in a board; in most cases, the grain follows the length of a board.

Grit: Refers to how densely a piece of sandpaper is coated with abrasive particles; the higher the grit number, the more and the finer the abrasive particles and the smoother the sanding action.

Groove: In tongue-and-groove paneling, a slot along the edge of one panel sized to accept the tongue on the edge of another panel.

H

Hardboard: A type of manufactured wood panel with smooth surfaces; made by gluing wood fibers together and forming them into panels.

Hardwood: Boards that are cut from deciduous (leaf-shedding) trees; hardwoods are usually but not always harder than softwoods.

K-L

Kerf: The cut created in wood by a saw blade.

Knot: A dark circle in a board formed by a branch growing from a tree's trunk. Unless a knot is loose, this defect does not affect the strength of a board.

Lap joint: A connection between two boards in which matching slots cut into the boards interlock.

M

Medium-density fiberboard (MDF): A manufactured wood product formed by gluing wood fibers together and forming them into panels.

Miter: An angled cut on a board—usually across the grain.

Molding: Strips of wood used to decorate a woodworking project.

N

Nail set: A cylindrical steel hand tool used with a hammer to sink the heads of protruding nails just below a wood surface.

Nominal size: The size of wood boards before they are smoothed at the sawmill. A 2x4, for example, is nominally 2 inches thick and 4 inches wide, but is actually 1 1/2 inches thick and 3 1/2 inches wide.

P

Pilot hole: A hole that makes it easier to drive a screw or nail and prevents the screw or nail from splitting the wood. Pilot holes are usually drilled a little deeper than one-half the length of the screw or nail. The diameter of the drill bit used should be slightly smaller than the diameter of the threaded part of the screw or the shaft of the nail.

Plywood: A type of manufactured panel made up of layers of wood veneer glued together. The grain direction of each layer runs at a 90-degree angle to the layers above and below, giving the panel its strength and stability.

R

Radius: The distance between the center of a circle and any point along its circumference or outside edge; the radius of a circle is one-half the diameter.

Rip cut: Sawing a board in the same direction as the wood grain—usually along the length.

S

Softwood: Boards that are cut from coniferous (cone-bearing) trees; some softwoods are actually harder than some hardwoods.

Spade bit: A drill bit with a flat section and a pointed end that comes in different sizes for drilling holes up to 1 1/2 inches in diameter.

Stain: A product for coloring wood.

Stop collar: An accessory for drilling a hole to a specified depth; the collar fits around the drill bit, allowing you to stop drilling when the collar contacts the wood.

T

Taper: An angled saw cut along the length of a board that reduces the width of the board progressively from one end to the other.

Tongue: In tongue-and-groove paneling, a protrusion along the edge of one panel that fits into the groove of another panel.

Twist: A defect in wood in which one or more parts of a board is warped.

V-W

Veneer: A thin sheet of wood, usually hardwood, glued down to a sheet of plywood; makes the plywood look like solid wood without the expense.

Warp: Any defect in wood that results in a board not being straight.

Wood filler: A product used to cover holes in wood; filler can be sanded and finished.

Index

Woodworking with Kids

Jean Angrignon Sirois, Clarisse Bériault, Joël Bériault,

Sylvie Bériault, Georges-Éric Caba, Minh Cao,

Jesse Carmichael, Alex Cassini-Brochu, Denis Chabot,

Lucien Chabot, Marie-Esther Chabot, Virgile Chabot,

Stéphanie Chayer, Sylvain Chayer, Mylène Faubert,

Camille Faubert-Gosselin, Adrienne Fournier-Sirois,

Dominique Gagné, Lise Gaudreault, Michel Giguère,

Hendley, Pierre Home-Douglas, Jason Hynes-Klempa,

Javel, Marie Joubert LeClerc, Stéphane Jutras,

Camille Jutras-Paquette, Robert Labelle, Minh Le,

Jérémie LeClerc, Marc-André Léger Chabot,

Kim Le Nguyen, Robert Lutes, Henriette Mailloux,

Magaëlle Mailloux-Houle, Geneviève Mantha,

Julien P. Galarneau, Léonie P. Galarneau,

Chantal Paquet, Jules Paquet-Régimbald, Josée Poirier,

Guy Prévost, Mathieu Prévost, Sonia Tevi

Picture Credits

Page 14: Courtesy Weyerhauser

Page 37: Courtesy Smithsonian Institute

Page 43: Courtesy Radio Flyer